Stirling Moss

The champion without a crown

Copyright © CHRONOSPORTS S.A., 2003

Jordils Park, Chemin des Jordils 40,
CH-1025 St-Sulpice,
SWITZERLAND
Tel.: (+41 21 694 24 44)
Fax: (+41 21 694 24 46)
E-mail: info@chronosports.com
www.chronosports.com

Printed and bound in Italy.

ISBN 2-84707-053-2

Stirling Moss
The champion without a crown

by

Pierre Ménard & Jacques Vassal

Car profiles
Pierre Ménard

Photographs
LAT (unless stated otherwise)

Translated from french by
Eric Silbermann

Design and cover
Cyril Davillerd

Layout
Tino Cortese, Cyril Davillerd

Contents

Stirling_MOSS

Prologue
Goodwood
23rd April 1962

As every year at Easter, the famous circuit in the heart of the countryside, near Chichester in the south east of England staged its "Easter Monday Trophy." The main event on the card was the "Glover Trophy," run over 100 miles for Formula 1 cars. For just over a year, the rules stated these cars must have a capacity of 1500 cc and a minimum weight of 450 kilos. 1961 had been a year of Ferrari domination and they had only been beaten twice, by Stirling Moss driving a Lotus entered by privateer Rob Walker. Now, the championship looked more open and the English constructors, particularly BRM and Lotus, had woken up, as had the private equipes. At the end of 1961, Stirling Moss had talked to Enzo Ferrari under a cloak of secrecy, which had reaped the promise of a Maranello Formula 1 car. It was to be painted in Rob Walker's colours; dark blue with a white band.

However, while awaiting delivery in time for the first round of the 1962 World Championship, at Zandvoort in the Netherlands, on 20th May, Moss and Walker had hatched a plan to run a different car for non-championship events like this one at Goodwood.

Stirling would drive a Lotus 18, updated to type 21 spec and, instead of the previous year's 4 cylinder engine, would run the new V8. The car belonged to Rob Walker, but for this event was entered in the light green colours of the UDT Laystall team.

The car did not run very well at the start of the year. On 1st April, in the Brussels Grand Prix,

Stirling took it to second place in the first heat, setting the fastest lap along the way, before having to retire in the second heat, with a broken camshaft. Then, on 14th April, in the Lombank Trophy at Snetterton, he set the fastest lap, but could only finish seventh, this time because of a stuck throttle.

This Easter Monday, Stirling was out for revenge, at least against mechanical frailties. All the more so, as he was particularly keen on the Goodwood circuit. In September 1948, aged nineteen he won a Formula 3 race here at the wheel of a Cooper. It was the first ever race at the circuit. In 1956, he won the Glover Trophy here with a Maserati. In August 1961, he had dominated the Tourist Trophy in a Ferrari 250 GT. Enough said; he knew the track like the back of his hand. Stirling (No. 7) was on pole position and alongside him albeit two seconds slower, was Graham Hill in a BRM. Moss pulled out an early lead, but he had to pit to adjust the gear change mechanism. Back on the track, he was now two laps down on the leader. No matter and true to habit, he set about climbing through the field, breaking the lap record on the way, a record he would share in the end with John Surtees, in 1'22". His climb was meteoric and, on lap 36, he had caught Graham Hill and was preparing to pass to unlap himself. But at that moment, for reasons still unexplained, Moss' Lotus veered left and flew off the track at nearly 200 km/h. It crossed the grass verge and piled into an embankment.

The rescue services arrived very quickly. The driver was seriously injured, with cranial injuries, a broken eye socket and multiple fractures to his arms and legs, as well as bruising. He had to be cut out of the wreckage, tangled in the twisted chassis rails which had trapped him in the car. It took forty five minutes to cut him free. Finally, Stirling, who had drifted into a coma, was taken to hospital in Chichester. Around one in the morning, his condition was deemed serious enough to warrant a transfer to the Atkinson Morley Hospital in Wimbledon. The long fight back to health had just begun.

Would Stirling Moss ever race again? For a whole year, this question would exercise the minds of everyone in racing. On 1st May 1963, after a long and tough convalescence, with a strict rehabilitation regime, Stirling once again got behind the wheel of a car; a Formula Sport Lotus 19, for a private test at the very same Goodwood circuit. But nothing would ever be the same again and Stirling announced his retirement to the press. Officially, it was the end of an extraordinary career, when he was at the very top of world motor sport. It would also be the start of another life... ■

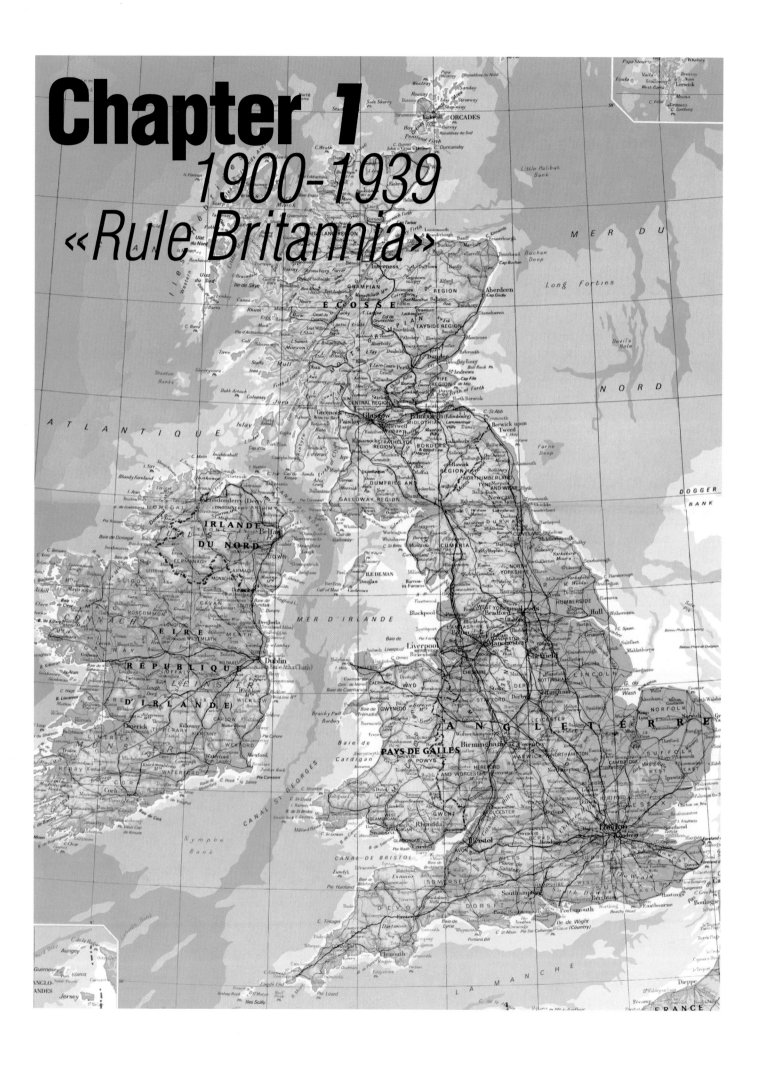

Chapter 1
1900-1939
«Rule Britannia»

Great Britain was a late starter when it came to the automobile. In 1900, the country could boast a mere 35,000 kilometres of roads, their layout dating back to the end of the eighteenth century and the start of the nineteenth. With the development of the automobile came more and better roads. In 1900, there were only 20,000 vehicles on the roads of Great Britain, but that figure shot up to 306,000 in 1931.

A major impetus to a future which would feature motoring for the masses was the abolition in 1896, of the famous "Locomotive Act." The first cars, were noisy, smoky and still a rare sight and they apparently scared the populace and their animals. Up to then, British law (it would be premature to talk of a Highway Code) meant that every motorist had to be preceded by a man walking along with a red flag! Once it was abolished, a group of enthusiasts set out at unlimited speed on a trip from London to Brighton (85 kilometres) to celebrate the event. The London to Brighton run went on to become a classic event, held every year on the first Sunday in November, for cars built prior to 1905. If motor racing has always been immensely popular in Great Britain it might owe something to the fact that it was born at the same time as this restriction was lifted. Add to this the traditional fighting spirit at the core of British life and one can understand how they soon managed to make up the initial deficit to the rest of continental Europe, especially France, which pioneered the sport. British marques, such as Humber, Napier and Wolseley were already famous. In 1907, the Brooklands autodrome was constructed in the south of England and would remain a major venue in world motor sport up to 1939, both for racing and for record breaking. Stirling's father, Alfred Moss, was a keen participant.

In 1909, the building and improvement of existing roads benefited from government funding to all the regions. In 1919, this work came under the auspices of the Department of Transport and in the 20s and 30s, 39,000 kilometres of what were known as

"Class I" roads were built, as well as 24,000 kilometres of "Class II" roads. The British car industry, as well as imported foreign makes had developed considerably. On the eve of the Second World War, when Stirling Moss was a ten year old youngster, Great Britain already had three million vehicles on its roads and their registration charges had helped finance the road building programme. Although the roads were heavily cambered, narrow and had no verges, just as many are to this day, the surface was better than that on the average European road. Even at this stage, many large towns and suburbs suffered from frequent traffic jams.

The United Kingdom of Great Britain and Northern Ireland (to give it its full title after the 1922 partition of Ireland) was a prosperous nation, proud of its army with a legendary navy and a civil and military airforce at the height of its powers. Of course, it also had its giant empire, the Commonwealth, which seemed indestructible. The population was gradually increasing thanks to a longer life expectancy and to the fact that emigration, notably Irish and Scottish, to the United States, Canada, Australia and New Zealand, was largely compensated for by a massive influx of immigrants from Europe (Italy, Germany and Spain) and colonies such as India. In 1939, almost 20 million workers, around a quarter of them women, were involved in the automobile industry and its suppliers. Most of the car and motorcycle business was centred in the Midlands, around Birmingham and Coventry.

In 1936, King Edward VII had abdicated, taking the title Duke of Windsor, giving up the prerogatives that went with sitting on the throne. He was succeeded by George VI, who reigned until 1952, when Queen Elizabeth II was enthroned. The monarchy was a central tenet of British life, with the monarch being the head of the Anglican Church. But the government was run by the Prime Minister with democratically elected members of parliament. The election of Members of Parliament to the House of Commons had been open to universal suffrage with the 1832 Reform Act, periodically amended to include

• 2_Henry Seagrave in a
Sunbeam at the ACF and
European Grand Prix, held at
Lyon on 3ʳᵈ August 1924. He
would have to settle for
5ᵗʰ place that day, but on
27ᵗʰ September, he won at
San Sebastian.
(DR)

all categories of the male population. It finally
entered the modern era in 1918, when thanks to
the Suffragette movement, run by militant
feminists of the day, women were also given the
vote as equals with their male counterparts.

Since time immemorial, political life was
dominated by the two main parties, the
Conservative Tories on the right and the Labour
Wigs on the left. The period between the two
wars saw a long-time Tory government. Eminent
politician Stanley Baldwin led the government
from 1924 to 1929 and again from 1935 to 1937.
In between, leadership fell to James Ramsey
McDonald from 1931. Baldwin was succeeded in
1937 by Neville Chamberlain, who was faced with
an extremely delicate diplomatic situation, which
saw him, accompanied by his French opposite
number, Edouard Daladier, go on a trip to Munich
to meet the Chancellor of the Third Reich, Adolf
Hitler. They returned with the famous "peace in
our time" paper, signed on 30ᵗʰ September 1938.
Despite the invasion of the Sudetan land and Nazi
Germany's annexation of Austria, Europe could
breathe again, or at least, that's what people
thought.

At this time, when Stirling Moss was a
young boy, the British featured strongly in various
sporting disciplines. Unfortunately, there were
precious few opportunities for their athletes to
shine in major international competitions, be they
athletics, cycling or even football. There were
exceptions, such as three British boxing world
champions: Jackie Brown (1932,) Benny Lynch
(1935) and Peter Kane (1938.) In tennis, Fred J.
Perry won the men's singles in the Davis Cup at
Wimbledon in 1934, 35 and 36, ending a long
period of American domination. In golf, the
Americans usually had the upper hand.

In motor sport, the English did much more
than make up the numbers, in part because the
car constructors were involved in high profile race
programmes. On two wheels, Norton set the
standard, winning on a regular basis at the Isle of
Man TT races in the 350 and 500 cc classes, as
well as winning various grands prix on the
continent. On four wheels, Bentley had long been
the dominant force, winning five Le Mans 24
Hours between 1924 and 1930. It was followed by
other marques such as Aston Martin, Lagonda and
MG. Lagonda also won the Le Mans 24 Hours in
1935. The two other marques specialised in the
smaller engine capacities, taking class wins at Le
Mans, as well as the Mille Miglia, the Spa 24
Hours and, of course, the Tourist Trophy.

That left the speed events, the international
grands prix, which the English then referred to in
French as the "Grandes Epreuves," which predated
the World Championship, only established in 1950.
The British constructors and drivers had yet to
make their mark in this discipline. One has to go
back to 1924 to find an English racer, Henry
Segrave, winning one of these events, the Spanish
Grand Prix at San Sebastian, in an English car, an
8 cylinder, two litre Sunbeam. After that and up to
the eve of the war, the best English drivers, like
Segrave, Lord Howe, Tim Birkin and Malcolm
Campbell had no competitive home-grown cars
and won on the international circuit at the wheel
of French cars, especially Bugatti, but also Talbot
and Delage, or Italian machinery (Maserati, Alfa
Romeo.) The legendary German Mercedes and
Auto Union were dominant at the time, but British
race fans only saw and heard them twice on home
soil, at the Donington Grands Prix in 1937 and
1938. They were memorable occasions, as one of
the Mercedes drivers was one of their own.

This British driver was a major player in pre-war grands prix with a meteoric rise to success. His name was Richard Seaman. Born in 1913, this talented young man with film-star good looks, made his debut in the "Voiturettes" category, evolved from that era's Formula 2 series, at the wheel of a venerable Delage. It boasted an 8 cylinder supercharged 1500 cc "Grand Prix" engine, dating from 1927, but heavily modified. With this old car he put on a bravura performance in the 1936 Eifel Cup at the Nürburgring and won four races, including the "Voiturettes" Grand Prix in Berne. His performances had come to the attention of the competitions manager of Mercedes-Benz, Alfred Neubauer. In 1936, Seaman raced as a privateer with a supercharged Alfa Romeo in some grands prix. In 1937, he signed with Mercedes as a works driver, which created a sporting and political sensation: an Englishman racing for a German team! Driving with skill and panache, Seaman was a flat out merchant and never considered cruising for a finish. In this, his temperament would be echoed by Moss, who would also race works Mercedes. Seaman had his first race for the team at Tripoli on 9th May 1937. He finished seventh and after this cautious debut, demanded by the redoubtable 645 horsepower W125, he began to challenge the team leaders, such as Caracciola, Lang and Von Brauchitsch, as well as their rivals

at Auto Union, Rosemeyer, Stuck, Hasse and Von Delius. The last mentioned sadly lost his life after crashing at the Nürburgring, where he had tangled with Seaman's Mercedes. At the Nürburgring again, the Englishman won the German Grand Prix on 24th July 1938. He was driving the Mercedes W 163, with a 3 litre V12 engine and it caused a sensation. He came second again in the Swiss Grand Prix and the Vanderbilt Cup, third at Donington and it established Seaman at the pinnacle of the sport. He met his fate at the 1939 Belgian Grand Prix at Spa, in a torrential downpour. Mounting a pointless pursuit of the leader, Muller in an Auto Union, he came into the corner before the La Source hairpin far too quickly. The Mercedes skidded went off the road and hit a sign and the car immediately burst into flames. Two brave marshals rushed to save the luckless driver. Unfortunately, as they did not know how to remove the steering wheel, they lost precious time. Seaman was badly burnt and died the following night in hospital. It was 25th June 1939.

A few weeks later, Europe would be embroiled in a bloody conflict for several years. No racing of course and life was no longer going to be "normal" for anyone. But life went on in England and notably for a young lad, who at the end of the war would become a robust adolescent with the first seeds of a champion. ∎

• **3**_Donington Park 1937. Richard Seaman in a Mercedes W 125 (no. 4) alongside Hermann Lang (Mercedes no. 2,) Bernd Rosemeyer (Auto Union no. 5) and Manfred Von Brauchitsch (Mercedes no. 3.) Rosemeyer went on to win the Donington Grand Prix.
(Photo Sport Général)

Chapter 2
1929-1940
The birth of the art

The Craufords are an old family, a Scottish clan with roots going back to the thirteenth century. Over the generations, its produced several strong personalities, who played their part in the country's history. Robert Crauford was the third son of the youngest branch of the family, from Kilburnie, an army officer who saw service in Latin America then Spain at the start of the nineteenth century. He became a General in the Light Division and was wounded in combat at Ciudad Rodrigo in 1812. Aged forty eight, he succumbed to his injuries a few days later.

Born on 7th July 1897 at Stirling, Aileen Crauford was the great grand niece of this General. The Craufords had moved to the South of England and Aileen spent her adolescence in Berkshire, surrounded by horses and she soon developed a lifelong passion for all things equestrian. An excellent horsewoman, she passed on this skill to her daughter, Patricia Ann and her son Stirling.

In the years from 1810 to 1820, a young Ashkenazy Jew, originally from Eastern Europe, was living in north London and was about to follow his parents' footsteps into business. He was called Abraham Moses. In 1832, he had a son called Nathan, who would go on to be an engineer. It was in London, at the Jewish College in Leadenhall Street that, on 29th August 1852, Nathan married the young and already pregnant Phoebe Abrahams. He was just twenty years old when he became the father of little Abraham, who took his grandfather's name. Abraham II, "Abe" to his friends, would enjoy a prosperous career as a property developer, buying and selling land to build on in the suburbs to match the development of the railways. In November 1878, aged twenty six, Abe married a slip of a girl of eighteen; a Christian by the name of Sarah Jane Durtnall. This event, along with the anti-semitism which existed in England as in the rest of the Europe at the time, drove him to anglicise his surname, as he started a family with Sarah Jane, which would grow to five children: Nathan was born in 1879, followed by Martha (1881,) Evelyn (1882,) their brother Ardon (1887) and finally Alfred (1896).

At the end of the nineteenth century, many Ashkenazy Jewish families fled poverty, famine and the pogroms in their home countries of Russia, Ukraine and Poland, to settle in Great Britain, creating a sort of lumpen proletariat. This led to problems with anti-semitism. On the other hand, Jewish families which were already integrated, some for over two centuries and now part of the bourgeoisie, wanted to disassociate themselves from the new arrivals. They had become part of a very conservative society, concerned with their status and maintaining strict social codes of class, ethnicity and religion. The parents in these families were worried, often quite rightly so as we will learn later, that their children, be it at school or at play, would be subject to bullying and mental and physical humiliation at the hands of their "goyim" (non-Jewish) peers. This meant that changing Jewish surnames was a common occurrence in the 1890s. Thus Abraham Moses dropped the "e" from his name; a move further prompted by the fact that, having married a Christian, his children would be raised outside the faith and customs of the Israelites.

Of these five youngsters, Alfred Ethelbert was the "Benjamin." From a very early age he showed an aptitude for manual work and more especially, anything mechanical. While his temperament could be described as lackadaisical, almost negligent, he was a strong character, who got things done; pragmatic, dynamic and entrepreneurial. During the Great War, while British soldiers were fighting in Europe, the young Alfred decided to take up dentistry, working as an assistant to a practising dentist. It was an eye-opening experience. He discovered that at the time, much of the British population, if suffering from cavities, would have their teeth pulled at a very early age. As for the women, they would often have their teeth removed and replaced with dentures, prior to marriage, to avoid future expense! Nevertheless, when Stirling's father became a dentist in the Twenties, his business quickly prospered and he ended up running several clinics.

• **4**_Alfred Moss at Brooklands in 1923, at the wheel of a 12 HP Crouch.

● **5**_Aileen and Alfred Moss in a Marendaz during a trial in the 1930s.

Interested in things mechanical other than teeth, Alfred took up motor sport. He was keen on originality and after trying a Motocar with two seats in tandem, he bought himself an Anzani-engined Crouch, which he raced at Brooklands, even taking a win at the legendary circuit. At this point, our young racer managed to persuade his father to finance a trip to the United States, to study at the School of Dentistry at the University of Indiana. It just happened to be located just a few blocks away from the famous "Brickyard," which every "Memorial Day" on 30th May staged the Indianapolis 500. From the moment he arrived in town to begin his studies in the Autumn of 1923, Alfred had but one thought in mind: to find a car to compete in the famous Indy 500 in 1924!

The young man certainly had some nerve, as he had only won one race in a very modest machine and, at this time, the 500 was already a major motor sport event, featuring battle hardened professional racers and some high class equipment. In those glorious far off days, the technical regulations were adopted from the European Grands Prix. The 1923 race had just been won by a two litre supercharged Miller, which had covered the 500 miles at an average speed of over 146 km/h, setting a lap record at over 176 km/h along the way. Apart from the American cars (Miller, Packard, Duesenberg,) there were some European cars on the grid, including Bugatti and Mercedes. Armed with a letter of recommendation from the British Mercedes importer for his American opposite number, Alfred Moss hoped to get his hands on one of these cars. But the German constructor had not entered a team in 1924, so Alfred had to look elsewhere. He struck lucky and found himself behind the wheel of a Barber-Warnock Special, which was actually a 4 cylinder Frontenac-Ford, designed by Louis Chevrolet. The car was out of its depth at this level, even if Henry Ford himself was the main sponsor. Nevertheless, Alfred managed to qualify on the penultimate row of the grid, at an average over the four flying laps allowed of 136 km/h. The pole time, set by an eight cylinder Miller averaged 173 km/h. Of 33 starters, 17 made it to the finish, with Alfred Moss 16th, 23 laps down on the winning Duesenberg. And so, the name of Moss appears in the records of this fantastic event, even though Stirling would never take part in it.

Back in England, with 900 dollars in prize money in his pocket, Alfred Moss joined forces with his brother-in-law to set up a Barber-Warnock dealership in Surrey, racing the cars at Brooklands. Not long after, he returned to dentistry and set up his first clinic in the east of London. But it was through motor racing that he would meet his future wife. At Brooklands, in 1926, he met Aileen Crauford who, while not abandoning her early passion for horses, had also developed an interest in things mechanical. It was love at first sight between the dentist and the young horsewoman.

Alfred and Aileen were married in 1927. Alfred decided to give up racing, but curiously his wife then decided to take it up! For safety reasons however, she opted for a less frenetic discipline than road racing, trying her hand at trials, endurance events and off-road trials. She drove a Marendaz, a now long forgotten English marque. These pretty cars, of which Aileen owned both a 1500 cc and 2 litre version, looked like a cross between a small Bentley and a big MG. With Alfred as navigator, Aileen won the British "Ladies" championship.

Their first child was a boy, born on 17th September 1929. Aileen wanted to call him Hamish, but Alfred reckoned that sounded too Scottish. The parents finally hit on the idea of naming him Stirling, after his mother's birthplace, to the north of Glasgow. At the time, the Moss family lived in a modest house in Thames Ditton. A nanny would look after little Stirling, while his parents competed in trials. But, in 1934, Aileen was pregnant again and Alfred found a more comfortable and spacious house at Bray, on the banks of the Thames. He borrowed to buy it and

● **6**_Stirling Moss' childhood home, the Long White Cloud.

● **8**_(facing page) Stirling on his pony, alongside his father. *"I did all this to please my parents, but it was a pain."*

called it "The Long White Cloud." It came with pastures and enough land to raise horses and other animals. Stirling and his little sister, Patricia Ann (Pat to her friends,) born in December 1934, would enjoy a happy childhood there.

In general, Alfred was a generous and none too authoritative father, although he did have a bee in his bonnet when it came to money. From a very early age, he instilled his children with a sense of values and worth, even though their lifestyle meant they were sheltered from any hardship. The children were not spoilt and Pat and Stirling were asked by their father to consider what they were prepared to give in exchange for whatever they were after. It was a lesson Stirling would not forget during his career as a racing driver.

A keen advocate of sport as part of the curriculum, Alfred taught Stirling to box when he was three years old. It would be a metaphor for the future, even if Alfred was unaware of that at the time. Stirling would soon need it to defend

himself. After attending nursery school at Shrewsbury House, Stirling became a boarder at Clewer Manor when he was seven. The headmaster was a rugby enthusiast and Stirling developed a passion for the oval ball game for a while. But thanks to his mother competing in trials and the beautiful Bentley which his father bought in 1939, Stirling was very much brought up in a motor sport environment.

That year, war broke out between Germany and France, allied to England. But war was a far off and abstract concept for a ten year old English boy. Ever ingenious, Stirling's father had designed and patented an air raid shelter. For Stirling, the main event of 1940 was the death of his grandfather, Abe. He also went through a succession of medical milestones; scarlet fever, appendicitis and a kidney inflammation, which kept him off school for a year. It was no hardship, as sitting at a desk bored him. He craved movement, preferably with an engine attached. ∎

● **7**_A very young Stirling with the family dog, Basher.

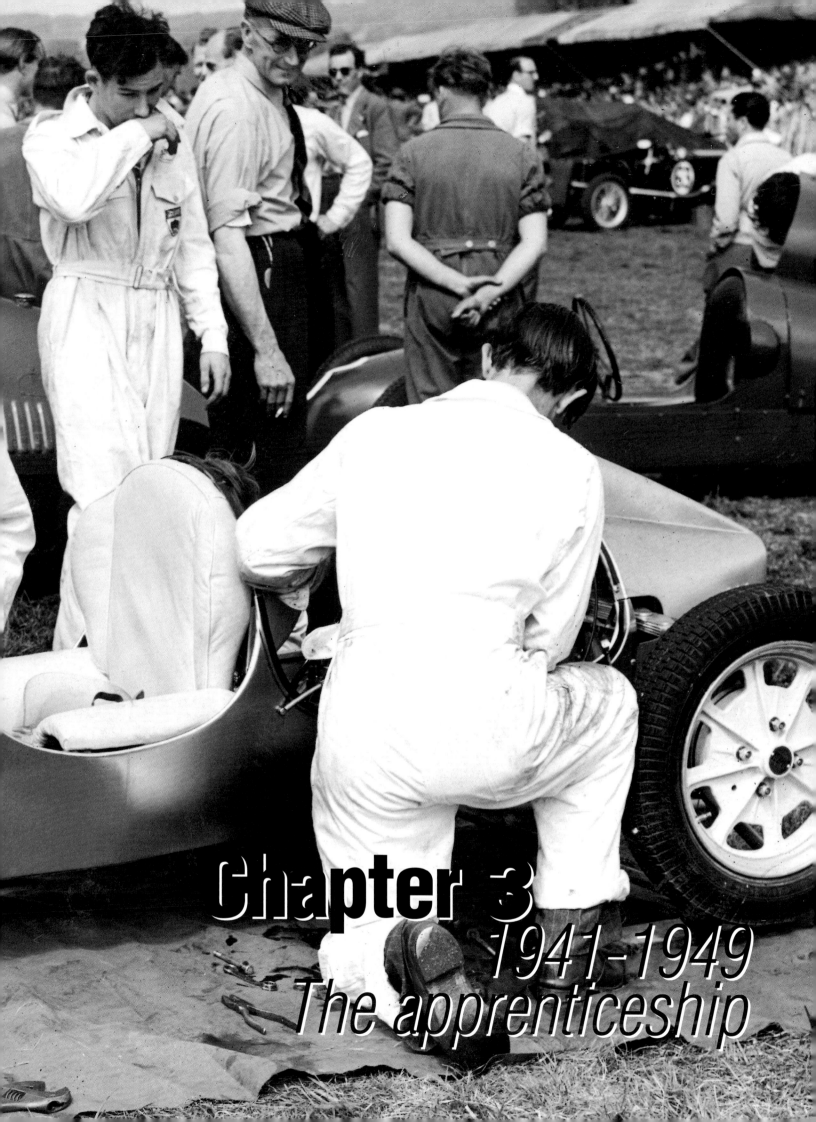

Chapter 3
1941–1949
The apprenticeship

• 10_Stirling and sister Pat, with their horses and a crop of show jumping trophies and rosettes.

We lived on a farm and my father had bought an old Austin Seven that we'd taken the body off for me to drive it round the grounds and to make it look more racy. Petrol was rationed. And then in 1945, I applied for my driving license. I was not even sixteen yet, which was the legal age, but they sent me one straight away. So I made use of it. After the

Austin, I had a 1936 Morgan three-wheeler with a Matchless engine. Then, when I was seventeen, my father bought me an MG TB coupe, one of the very last pre-war models. And then I wanted to race. At first, my father was against it." During this interview, which took place in Monaco in 2002, Sir Stirling Moss – he had recently been knighted by Prince Charles, having been

went to Haileybury in Hertfordshire, to the north of London. *"I was good in maths, but I didn't like Latin or History. So I turned to woodwork, I was not a brilliant scholar."* At Haileybury, Stirling learned another hard lesson, a social one this time. Anti-Semitism was rife amongst his fellow pupils. He had to put up with insults about his father's origins and it was all the more hurtful for being unexpected. These days, it is not a subject he discusses openly, but when questioned about it, he is prepared to offer a frank reply. *"Yes it's true, I suffered because I am antagonistic by nature. I did not consider myself Jewish because my mother, being Scottish, used to take me to church. As for my father, it had never dawned on me until then that he was Jewish. I never really accepted it and I had to fight at school and came up against a lot of opposition."*

Stirling occasionally got into fights at school and it proved a sad way for his boxing skills to be used. But he never spoke of these problems with his father; neither then, nor later. To his dying day, which came in 1974, when Stirling was 45, Alfred was unaware of the hardships which had forged his son's fighting spirit. *"I had two or three good friends at school and occasionally I would bring them home. They never spoke about what went on and I never felt it was right to bring these problems home. My mother knew nothing about it and neither did my sister. I was not very close to Pat when we were children. I was seven when she was born. My mother was delighted, but for me...she was just a girl. A fifteen year old boy has no interest in a kid. It was only later, when we were adults that we really got to know one another."*

However, they did have one thing in common from childhood: horse riding. Aileen inculcated the siblings with her passion for horses, albeit more successfully with Pat than with her brother. As Stirling admitted bluntly: *"I did it to please my mother, but it was a pain. She made us do it, so I couldn't say no. When Pat was about two or three, they sat her on a pony with a little saddle and at six she started jumping. That put me under pressure, so I did it too."*

honoured in the Queen's 2000 New Year's Honours List – he was true to his reputation and wanted to rush through his memoirs at the same speed he lived his life. We had to bring him back; back to his family, his adolescence and to Stirling before the days of racing. In 1943, aged 14 the young man went to the Imperial Service College, which was a feeding ground for the military. He

● **9**_Previous double page. Goodwood, 19th April 1949: an engine change on Moss' Cooper-Jap Mk II. Stirling is standing behind the car. Kneeling next to him, Don Muller. In the front, the V twin 1000 cc Jap engine with which Stirling won that day's Easter Handicap, having set the fastest time in qualifying. In the other race, his 500 cc single cylinder blew its piston! *(The Autocar Editorial)*

Planet News Ltd

Pat Moss:
"I beat him... in a running race!"

A great rally champion and wife of the famous Swedish rally driver Eric Carlsson (on left in photo on their wedding day in London in 1963,) Pat Moss recalls:
"Stirling and I took part in gymkhanas and show jumping competitions. I was in the British team for 15 years, competing at international level. I was not professional but they were high level competitions. When I was little, I hated cars. Then, one day, Ken Gregory (Stirling's manager) was due to take part in a fun rally, a sort of treasure hunt and he said *'why don't you come along?'* I did and I enjoyed myself. I started rallying in 1954. I had a Triumph TR2, then I switched to MG. Stirling also did a bit of rallying, but he concentrated on circuit racing. It's a totally different world. One day in 1955, he brought me to Silverstone with an MGA, to see how I was braking. I was braking too early and lifting off at least 100 metres before the braking zone. He showed me the right braking distances and how to brake. He said, *'whatever you do, don't lift off, you're not on a Sunday drive! You must either accelerate or brake, but nothing in between.'* I was grateful for the advice and it helped me a lot. I remember one incident at Sebring in 1960. I was racing for BMC. We ran Austin-Healey Sprites. Stirling's had a slipping clutch, so as a good sister I let him take mine which was working properly and I took the other one. But at the 'Le Mans' type start, I ran quicker than him and started first. I was very proud of that!"

Together, the brother and sister spent several years on the show jumping circuit, often winning trophies and even money. Sometimes the prize-money would be as much as ten pounds, a considerable sum for a young man in 1945 and '46. Stirling won enough to open his own bank account in which to keep his savings. It would serve to realise his dream of buying his first racing car. Around this time, Charles Cooper, a Surbiton garage owner and former Brooklands mechanic, had just built, with help from his son John, his first 500 cc single-seater. It was made up of two Fiat Topolino chassis, cut in half, with two sections then welded together, a single cylinder 500 cc motorcycle engine mounted in the rear, a Triumph gearbox and chain drive. The body was panel beaten aluminium and there it was –a junior formula. From 1947, this British invention, Formula 500 would evolve into Formula 3, recognised at international level by the FIA, as a stepping stone to the 2 litre Formula 2 class and the brand new Formula 1 class (1500 cc supercharged or 4.5 litre normally aspirated.) A new generation of drivers would emerge from

this melting pot, many going on to become the leading players in motorsport in the Fifties; Collins, Hawthorn, Schell etc.

And of course, Moss himself. Aged 17, Stirling was a works Cooper driver, on a salary of 50 pounds, a fact which Alfred was unaware of. What happened next? Stirling told us in London, in July 1986. *"My father found the cheque book and asked me what this fifty pound deposit was. So, I had to tell him and he wrote to the company saying:* 'My son is too young and does not have permission to race'. *The money went back and my Morgan three-wheeler was confiscated! I had to get around on a bicycle, which was a backward step, because when you are going out with a girl, it helps to have a car!"* His father cited the high costs of racing as, not only did one need a competitive car, it had to be prepared, a mechanic needed to be paid and there were travel costs involved. As for Aileen, she was worried about the dangers of the job. Finally, a compromise was reached. In 1947, Stirling was allowed to take part in sprints and autotests at the wheel of a BMW 328 bought and entered by his father. Stirling admits that, while handling the 2 litre six cylinder car quite well, he never got the most out of it. Nevertheless, he finished first in a trial in Harrow on 2ⁿᵈ March 1947 and first in class at Eastbourne on 28ᵗʰ June. Then, while waiting to race for real, he went on a hotel management course in London, training as a barman, receptionist and porter. He was paid 30 shillings per week, for working nights and weekends and having to rent a room, he was losing money and soon got fed up with the arrangement. His father then suggested he return to the farm at Bray, where he would have to work 48 hours a week and get up very early. He hated it, but it was a price he was prepared to pay for free weekends and the hope of racing.

Towards the end of 1947, having dragged his father to gawp in front of the showroom of the Surbiton garage, Stirling finally got parental agreement to buy a Cooper-Jap Mk II from the factory. The little single-seater cost 575 pounds, which was a good deal less than some of the thoroughbred ponies with which Stirling and Pat won show-jumping events. This time, not only was Alfred agreeable to the deal, he entered wholeheartedly into the project.

Having known the people from Jap since his Brooklands days, he helped his son track down a Jap engine. Then he adapted one of his horse trailers to take a racing car. A German farmhand,

Don Muller worked for the Moss family and was given the job of race mechanic for the Moss team. The first test took place very near Bray on the tarmac roads of a building site. Joining Alfred and Don Muller in supervising the operation was Charles Cooper, who personally delivered the car. The constructor was immediately impressed with Stirling's style, in terms of the easy way in which he handled the car and his application; all the hallmarks of a great professional driver of the future.

With all elements in place, Stirling tackled his first real racing season in 1948. The Cooper was entered in his name, painted in a cream colour with a stirrup motif, harking back to his equestrian past (and the transporter taking him to the track!) His baptism of fire took place at the Prescott Hillclimb, home to the British Bugatti Club, which accepted a variety of categories. On this legendary course, of around 1100 metres in length, Stirling set the fourth quickest time in his class, in 51"01. He made rapid progress and on 18ᵗʰ July, at the same venue, he won his class in 49"5. There were other events in between these two. Most significantly, he made his track debut at the Brough aerodrome on 7ᵗʰ April, when he won his heat, the final and the handicap race, as well as doing the best qualifying lap and setting the fastest race lap! He beat drivers who had already earned their spurs, including Bob Gerard,

● **11**_15ᵗʰ July 1948: Stirling wins the Bouley Bay hillclimb with his Cooper-Jap 500 Mk II, setting a new outright record in 63"80.
(The Autocar Editorial)

who made his name at the wheel of a supercharged ERA and the fact Stirling was so young made an impression on the racing community. In September, Stirling won the inaugural three lap race at Goodwood, at an average speed of 115.7 km/h, once again beating the best experts.

In 1949, still with the support of his father, Stirling decided to try and move up the ladder. In order to be spotted by professional teams, in the hope of landing a works drive, it would be essential to race in the bigger categories like Formula 2 and Formula Libre and to gamble on competing further afield. With this in mind, the Moss' bought a new Cooper, the Mk III, which could be fitted with either a 500 cc Formula 3 engine or a 1000 cc twin cylinder, eligible in Formula 2. After winning a five

lap handicap race at Goodwood in April with the 1000 engine, then a Formula 3 race in May, as a curtain-raiser to the British Grand Prix at Silverstone, taking the fastest race lap in both, Stirling set off to make his continental debut in July. It was off to Italy to start with. It was his first trip to the Lake Garda circuit, a difficult and dangerous track. 16 kilometres in length, it boasted 75 corners, including a series of hairpins and downhill sections. The race was run over two elimination heats and a final, each 110 kilometres in length. Stirling was up against the big guns like Villoresi, Tadini and Sterzi, driving Ferraris. He finished third in his heat, much to the delight of an enthusiastic Italian crowd and to the dismay of local stars like Clemente Biondetti, a four times winner of the Mille Miglia no less. Stirling drafted

past his 2 litre V6 Ferrari 166 right in front of the pits. In the final, Stirling came third with this little "spider" with a motorbike engine which, only a few hours earlier had almost been laughed out of the paddock. He picked up the equivalent of 200 pounds in prize money, but more importantly, made a big impression on the organisers. *"At first, we were brought in just to fill up the grids, but I realised that if I waved at the spectators crowded round the track, they waved back and the organisers said to themselves: 'Well, he seems popular, so let's bring him back next year'. That way I was paid more the next year."*

On 17th July at Reims, he entered the Coupe des Petites Cylindrees, as a curtain-raiser to the French Grand Prix. Unfortunately, his chain let him down during the race. But, on 31st July in Holland,

on his first trip to Zandvoort, he scored a great win. In August in Lausanne, he got the trophy for "the most deserving performance" for his stunning race debut, despite retiring with an engine failure.

All these showing, with or without a result to show for it at the end, were being to make the professionals sit up and take notice. Of course there were some mealy-mouthed rivals who reckoned Moss was pushing too hard. One of these days, predicted the prophets of doom, he would crash and that would calm him down. What they were unaware and what the man in question would only admit to years later, was that he was still driving well within his own limits! However, a team boss spotted Moss' true potential and signed him up for 1950. His name? John Heath. His cars? HWM. ■

• **12**_Silverstone, 2nd October 1948: Stirling leads the field through Woodcote in the 500 race, a curtain raiser to the British Grand Prix. Having beaten the class record in 3'17"4 (average 66.98 mph,) he retired with a broken gearbox pinion.
(The Autocar Editorial)

Chapter **4**
1950
In at the deep end

My father helped me a lot, I must say. We were doing a one kilometre hillclimb and he would strip the heads on the Jap engine and check the valves, so he was heavily involved. And when John Heath offered me a contract, my father did not object in the slightest. John offered me 25% of the start money and the prize money, so when we had a bit of luck, that would bring in about 200 pounds a race. That was enough to live on, but I was travelling from one circuit to another in John's 15 Citroen, I was staying in cheap hotels and I bought something to eat along the way. It was a marvellous period, when we lived a bit like gypsies. After the race, we would go to the party to pick up our prize money and we often had a good time!"

John Heath and his partner, George Abecassis, had a garage in Walton on Thames in Surrey, not far from Brooklands. It went by the name of Hersham & Walton Motors. Both men were semi-professional racers driving Altas and even a Bugatti 59. Abecassis also drove Aston Martins in endurance races. In 1948, they built a "special," then in 1949 came the first HW Alta, a two-seater which raced in Formula 2, Sports cars and even Formula Libre. It was based around a two-seater open car and the mudguards and lights were removed or replaced to suit each category. It was the sort of thing that could be done in those days and was an effective cost saving measure. With a lot of racing taking place in Europe, organisers needed to fill their grids and one car, slightly modified, could qualify for two events. In 1950, the Walton on Thames garage built three identical cars, which were named HWM, based on a home-built chassis, as always fitted with Alta 4 cylinder 2 litre engines, putting out 140 horsepower and fitted with a pre-selector Armstrong-Siddeley gearbox. It was a system already fitted to pre-war ERAs and MGs and in France (Wilson gearbox) on the Talbot-

• **13**_Goodwood, 26ᵗʰ March 1951: first race first win for Moss' new HWM. It's the Lavant Cup which only went on for five laps, but Moss beat Eric Brandon (Cooper 1100 cc) and Lance Macklin driving the other HWM was fourth.

● **14**_The two seater HWM, like some Ferraris and Maseratis of that era, could race in Formula 2, Formula Libre and Formula Sport. It was Moss' weapon for his first encounters with the Grand Prix drivers.

Lago. A lever fitted underneath the steering wheel allowed the driver to pre-select any given gear, which was then only selected at the opportune moment, by pressing the clutch pedal, which offered a degree of driving sophistication which Stirling much appreciated. "*It left both hands free to drive the car in the braking area and while cornering. I found it an advantage on twisty tracks, where the disadvantages of its weight and the way it sapped power were minimised.*" Moss first tested the HWM in December 1949, at a private test session at the Odiham aerodrome. Unfortunately, he went off the track, putting a hole in the sump, returning disgruntled to the pits. John Heath did not make a meal of it, knowing he had a young charger on his hands.

That year, the HWM team was made up of John Heath himself, Moss and Lance Macklin, a more experienced driver, whom Stirling recalls thus: "*Lance was ten years older than me. His father was one of the founders of Invicta. Lance was an Olympic skier and an excellent all-round sportsman, a well educated man who was very*

successful with the ladies. I learnt a lot from him, not just about racing, but about life in general. We spoke about all sorts of things together; for example about John Heath, who had a girlfriend we didn't think much of, on whom he spent the money that should have gone on the cars. Our team ran on a very tight budget. Alf Francis, the chief mechanic was very poorly paid. We would arrive in a town and he would find a garage where he would ask a local lad to lend a hand."

Alf Francis, real name Kovalevski, was a Polish refugee who was very smart and resourceful. In fact, he was the one who built the HWMs. Later he would become Stirling's personal mechanic and also a close personal friend. Stirling did not touch the cars, leaving that to the expert. He was not very interested in the technical side. "*We raced what we were given,*" he recalled laconically. Even driving technique remained rudimentary. "*At first I didn't even know what oversteer or understeer were.*" Stirling reckons he learnt a lot on the job, watching others, while he raced the HWM with which he first came across the great champions like Ascari,

Ken Gregory: "Stirling needed to be contradicted"

"At the time, I was issuing racing licenses for the 500 Club as well as doing a bit of racing myself. At this dinner, we were on the same table as Peter Collins. We talked about our various projects. Stirling lived in Maidenhead and I had a flat in London. I suggested he move in with me as it would be a more practical base in between the races. We immediately became friends that night. At the end of 1951, it became obvious that he would become a professional driver. I spoke to him and his father about it and I became Stirling's manager. We never had a contract, it was just a handshake between friends. And it stayed like that until 1964. We always trusted one another, which did not mean there weren't plenty of arguments. In fact, Stirling needed to be contradicted. He didn't want everyone to agree with him. He has always been very competitive in all aspects of his life. When it came to reaching an agreement, he was always trying to get the best out of it. I worked with Alfred Moss, his father, who helped a lot. We tried to ensure that not all three of us be in the same place at the same time to leave a margin for negotiation."

Fangio and Farina. The latter in particular made a strong impression, because of his style, his upright stance, arms extended, precise and elegant. But Giuseppe (known as "Nino") Farina who in 1950 became the first ever Drivers' World Champion at the wheel of a supercharged Alfa Romeo 158, was also a tough and merciless adversary. *"He was quick, but he could be nasty. I tried to copy his style just for appearances sake."* A surprising remark from a driver who was always nothing but correct on track, which was not always the case with the Italian champion. But Moss can handle a paradox and he had a highly developed sense of the aesthetics of it all with panache being almost as important as the result. This streak is why his racing kit (white helmet, white overalls, later replaced by light blue ones) was always immaculate and why he always had a wave for a photographer friend or the crowd at the side of the track. For Moss, racing was not just a sport and a job, it was a spectacle and it had be good to watch, so that the public wanted to come again and the organisers would invite him back!

To develop his blossoming career, he needed a manager. Commonplace these days, it was a rare move at the time. Moss met Ken Gregory, then the secretary of the 500 Club, in 1949 at an end of season Formula 3 dinner in London. Ken recalled what happened back then (see box above.)

It was during the 1950 season that all the loose ends came together for Stirling, as he learnt his trade while bringing his personal touch to the job. He also encountered the opposition (the Ferraris and often, the agile Simca-Gordinis, well driven by Manzon, Trintignant and Simon) and got to grips with the main European circuits. After Goodwood on 6th April, a trip to Montlhery ended with a retirement because of a broken con rod. At Mons, in Belgium, he finished seventh, while the Belgian, Johnny Claes, won in an HWM and at Aix-les-Bains, he retired because of... indigestion! Luckily, in between these races, Moss won with his new Cooper-Jap Mk IV in the Formula 3 races at Silverstone and then at Monaco, the latter event a curtain raiser for the Formula 1 Grand Prix, in front of all the key players. But the time had come to get to grips with Formula 2. On 11th June, in Rome, at the Thermes de Caracalla circuit, Stirling made a big impression. Running third on the heels of the factory Ferraris driven by Ascari and Villoresi, he had just set the fastest race lap, much to the delight of an enthusiastic Italian crowd, when a front wheel came off his HWM. Stirling managed to stop in extremis on three wheels and unhurt. He was carried back to the pits shoulder high by the fans! There was brief interlude back home before returning to the continent. It was just time enough to win five Formula 3 races at Brands Hatch on 25th June (a heat, the "open" final, another heat and the "production" final and a race for the ten quickest drivers in the previous finals, plus the lap record and all on the same day!)

At Reims on 2nd July, he came third in the Jean-Pierre Wimille Cup (Formula 2) in the HWM, behind Ascari (Ferrari) and Simon (Simca-Gordini.) Better still, one week later at Bari, in a Formula 1 race this time, he finished third ahead of Levegh's Talbot, Cortese's Ferrari 166 S and a pack of Maserati CLTs, but just behind the Alfettas of Farina and Fangio. Over half a century later, Moss still savours the moment. "*It was my first important result at this level of competition. The organisers had accepted the HWM to swell the field and it turned out that I went well that day, right behind the Alfettas which were fearsome cars. I remember a moment when Farina went wide while passing me going into a corner and I got him back down the inside. Fangio, who was following him closely, then went past me and he turned to me with a big smile, pointing at Farina who had got it wrong. That was my first encounter with Fangio.*" It was also the day that the "Commendatore" Enzo Ferrari first took note of the very quick "inglese."

Not all the races were such fun. A fortnight later in Naples, at the Posilippo circuit, Moss and his HWM won the heat and set the fastest lap. He was leading the final when he came up behind a backmarker who waved him through. At the critical moment the slower car ran wide and a wheel nut punctured a tyre on the HWM, which was in a full four wheel drift at over 130 km/h at the time. Moss was unable to keep control and the car hit a tree. Stirling cracked a kneecap under the dashboard and broke several teeth. He had the presence of mind to get out of the car, but he only managed a couple of metres before fainting. Later, he would say he had thought of Dick Seaman, trapped uninjured in his Mercedes until it burst into flames. Alfred Moss was immediately told the news and jumped on a plane to bring his son home and to fix his broken teeth. Fifteen days later, just about on his feet again, Stirling was back at the wheel at Brands Hatch in Formula 3 (1st in his heat and 2nd in the final with the lap record.) Then in August and September, it was back to the HWM in Berne, Silverstone and Mettet in Belgium.

In the meantime, his career would take a step forward. This time it was due to sports and endurance racing, a discipline in which he was still a novice, but was soon to become a master. Nevertheless, apart from HWM, which cancelled its sports car programme through lack of funds, the factory teams were not interested. For the Tourist Trophy, being held for the first time at Dundrod in Northern Ireland on 16th September, Stirling was looking for a drive. He was turned down one by one by Aston Martin, Jaguar and even MG. "*They thought I was a car breaker,*" he explained. In the end he was berthed by privateer Tommy Wisdom. "*Tommy was a journalist with the Daily Herald. He had raced a bit at Brooklands before the war and he knew my parents. He was offered a Jowett Jupiter for the Tourist trophy, having just bought a Jaguar XK 120. He rang me and offered the Jaguar for the TT. It was a fabulous opportunity.*"

The Jaguar was one of six aluminium-bodied specials sold to hand-picked customers. Tommy suggested splitting the start and prize money with Stirling 50/50. A few days before the Mettet race in the HWM, Stirling tested a standard XK 120, lent to him by the factory at

the insistence of Tommy Wisdom. After Mettet, he flew to Belfast. He arrived in Dundrod determined to prove his doubters wrong. On this dangerous, narrow and twisty circuit, he and the Jaguar would work miracles. The first practice session was held in the rain and Moss lapped in 6'05" as against 5'39" for Leslie Johnson in an identical car. The next day, in the dry, Moss did a 5'28" as he got used to the car. The race was held in a downpour which lasted three hours. Leslie Johnson set off in the lead, but right from the second lap, Stirling passed him. He maintained the lead, increasing it right to the last lap. It was first international endurance win on the eve of his twenty his first birthday. As a birthday present it was worth 1400 pounds in prize money, a considerable sum in 1950. But more importantly, it also prompted Jaguar boss William Lyons to sign him up as the number one driver for 1951.

To round off this busy and promising season, after a few more races with the HWM and a Formula 3 Cooper (Perigueux, Goodwood, Castle Combe and Lake Garda,) Stirling was invited by Jaguar to take part in several publicity

stunts involving record breaking at Montlhery. On 24th and 25th October, at the legendary autodrome, Leslie Johnson and Stirling took turns at the wheel, each driving for three hours, completing a 24 hour run at an average speed of 172.9 km/h. It was to launch the Jaguar XK 120 as a legendary sports car. Moss was back at Montlhery again in August 1952, sharing driving duties with Jack Fairman, Bert Hadley and Lesley Johnson, at the wheel of a bronze coloured factory coupe. They drove non-stop for an entire week at an average of 161 km/h!

The indefatigable Moss was also at Montlhery in November 1950, this time with Ken Gregory, the dilettante driver who would become his manager. They brought a new single-seater, the Kieft, fitted with a Manx Norton engine. They beat six records in the 350 cc international class "J" and seven others from 50 to 200 miles at average speeds of 140 to 144 km/h. A great racing career had shot into orbit and with his incredible versatility there was plenty more to come. ■

● **16**_Dundrod,
16th September 1950: the Tourist Trophy in a Jaguar XK 120 special, kindly lent by Tommy Wisdom for Stirling's first international win. In the pouring rain, he displayed commendable maturity. It was the eve of his 21st birthday.

● **17**_Goodwood, 14th May 1951: Moss receives the Glover Trophy from Mrs. Glover. He had just won the Formula 3 final in a Kieft-Norton which was making its debut that day.

Chapter 5

1951-1953
Looking for the right Formula

Hot on the heels of his victory in the Tourist Trophy at the wheel of an XK 120, in 1951, Moss would carve out a reputation as the supreme master of endurance racing. Helping him on his way was a new weapon developed by the Jaguar engineers, led by Wally Hassan: the XK 120 C open seater, later known as the C type. It used the famous XK straight six block, with two overhead camshafts which, along with the Colombo-designed Ferrari 60 degree V12, was the most successful Sports and Grand Touring engine. Two different schools of thought, both sharing the same concerns of reliability, versatility, sale to privateers and the possibility for long-term development. The result was that, between them, they powered some of the most beautiful road cars of the age, winning regularly in the toughest endurance races, such as the Le Mans 24 Hours, the Reims 12 Hours, the Tourist Trophy and the Tour de France.

The Jaguar C type had a 3442 cc engine, putting out around 200 horsepower (220 for the later models.) It was an open two-seater, with a tubular chassis distinguished by a glut of curves, the work of Malcolm Sayer, who later created his masterpiece in the form of the D type. It had a top speed of over 240 km/h with long gearing and the drivers appreciated its handling, particularly on fast tracks like Le Mans and Reims. The first ones to be built were prototypes for the factory team, run by "Lofty" England. Shortly after, a small production run of around fifty cars was built. As had been the case with the XK 120, Tommy Wisdom was one of the first to get his

hands on one. Apart from a few lapses, Moss would enjoy enormous success with the C type. Those lapses were sometimes down to poor preparation, as was the case in the 1951 Le Mans 24 Hours, when copper oil pipes failed on two or three of the factory cars, including the Moss/Fairman machine which was leading at the time, on lap 92. The third car (Walker/Whitehead) made it to the finish, giving Jaguar its first win at the Sarthe circuit. Small consolation for Moss, he beat the lap record in the early part of the race, when he was fighting off Gonzalez in the Talbot. In May 1952, he did the Mille Miglia with Jaguar's test driver, Norman Dewis as co-driver and the Jaguar C was fitted with disc brakes, first tried at Goodwood in April. Contrary to popular opinion, it was not an instant panacea. Moss recalled that sometimes, including during practice for Le Mans, the brake fluid would surge and the driver would find himself braking for a corner and the pedal would go straight to the floor. A guaranteed cold sweat! In the Mille Miglia, Moss was given plenty to think about when, in the rain, with strong crosswinds, he was overtaken near Ravenna by a Mercedes 300 SL. Moss later retired in Brescia with broken rear suspension and a holed fuel tank and he was worried about Le Mans. He said to Lofty England, "*we need more top speed.*" So the team manager hurriedly ordered up bodies with a sharper nose, reputedly worth an extra 10 to 15 km/h down the long straights like the Hunaudieres. What he had not counted on was the engines overheating. The Jaguars retired, Levegh's Talbot led for a long time before retiring

● **19**_Monaco, 2nd June 1952: in the Jaguar C type, Moss was chasing Robert Manzon's Gordini 2.3l in a Formula Sport race. At Sainte Devote, Manzon skidded on a patch of oil dropped by Parnell's Aston Martin and Moss went off right behind him. He was helped back on track by spectators and therefore disqualified. *(The Autocar Editorial)*

in the 23rd hour, leaving the Mercedes 300 SLs to take an unexpected one-two finish. Between these two events came the Monaco Grand Prix on 2nd June, run unusually as a Formula Sport event. Moss and his Jaguar C should have won, but a huge shunt at Sainte-Devote prevented it. Parnell's Aston Martin DB 3 dropped a con-rod and poured oil over the track. Robert Manzon in the Gordini skidded on the puddle and hit the Aston. Then Moss also skidded in the Jaguar. It could never happen today, but back then, national pride saw English spectators leap over the straw bales to help their champion straighten out a wing which was rubbing on a wheel. Moss hobbled away again, stopped at the pits for repairs, but he was disqualified for receiving "outside assistance."

Moss was equally unlucky come the 1953 Mille Miglia, this time with Morris-Goodall as his co-driver. They retired with a broken axle. "*Lofty England was not as good a team manager as John Wyer or Alfred Neubauer,*" confided Moss. "*When we asked for improvements to the Jaguar, for example, separate bucket seats or an additional fuel tank for the C type for the Mille Miglia, he always invoked his 'experience,' which he used as a pretext for not getting things done.*"

There were successes of course. On 15th September 1951, Moss won the Tourist Trophy, again at Dundrod and again in the pouring rain and to make his point, he set the fastest lap in qualifying, won the race and took the team prize. In June 1952 he won a race of over 400 km at Reims, in one of Tommy Wisdom's

Robert Manzon: "I gifted him a few"

Robert Manzon, from Marseille, was a very quick driver, at the wheel of Gordinis, Lancias and Ferraris. But he is relatively unknown even though he played in the big league. He has clear memories of Monaco in 1952 and of Moss in particular.

"*On Saturday, in the small capacity race, I won with a Simca-Gordini 1500 and he had a Frazer-Nash. I had just overtaken him and I thought I was first as he had been in the lead all the time! The next day, I had a 2.3 litre car. Moss set off in the lead, but I quickly got past him. Of course, he hung on behind me! We both skidded on oil from the Aston Martin as the marshals did not react very quickly. But I would not have lasted much longer as my steering was beginning to seize up. Moss was a very tough opponent. I gifted him a few races, for example at Reims where I hit a pylon while leading. Then there was Sebring in '54, where I was sharing a Lancia with Taruffi. We broke down one hour from the finish, but we were not classified as our car was no longer running. But we had completed more laps than him in the little Osca. For me, Moss was a real gentleman and demonstrated fair play in every sense of the word. He was a very pleasant chap, but the fact that he spoke very little French and I spoke no English limited our friendship.*"

(Photo Christian Bedei)

• **20**_Dundrod, 5th September 1953: last refuelling for the C type Jaguar of Moss, in the white helmet and Peter Walker, sitting on the wall in white overalls, on the way to 4th overall and 1st in the over 3 litre class of the Tourist Trophy. *(The Autocar Editorial)*

Jaguar C types, taking the lead after Robert Manzon crashed his Gordini because of a broken stub axle. The Frenchman jumped from the cockpit while the car was still moving, leaving the little 2.3 litre car to wreck itself against a pylon! Moss used the same car to win a couple of events at Boreham and Turnberry. In 1953, driving a works C type, he finished second at Le Mans with Peter Walker, behind the victorious Tony Rolt and Duncan Hamilton. Then with Peter Whitehead, Moss won the Reims 12 Hours. Privately though, he admitted he did not enjoy the long endurance races, as he did not like racing as a team, sharing

the car with another driver, as well as having to run at reduced pace. For example, the Jaguar C type's rev limit was dropped from the 6100 rpm used in the sprint events to 5500. "*In my opinion that's not racing,*" he reckoned. "*I want to be able to push myself to the limit.*"

So Moss turned to single seaters to fully express his talent, starting with a full season of Formula 3 races, at the wheel of a Norton powered Kieft. The car was built for him by a Welsh industrialist, Cyril Kieft, based on drawings by Dean Delamont and built by Ray Martin. Ken Gregory and Stirling got involved in the project.

• **21**_In 1952, Moss and the Kieft-Norton, carrying the lucky number 7, took three Formula 3 wins from three starts. Then he finished third at Silverstone at the BRDC meeting on 10th May. The car was destroyed in a collision in Brussels in the Cambre woods.

The Kieft's distinguishing feature was its very far forward driving position and, according to Moss, it was also the first car to use different suspension settings for each circuit. Moss won at Goodwood, Silverstone, Zandvoort and Brands Hatch in 1951. At the Nürburgring, in the curtain raiser for the Grand Prix, he shattered the lap record by 40 seconds! He also won the Fribourg hillclimb in 8'18", 31 seconds quicker than Ken Wharton in a 1000 cc Cooper-Jap. In 1952, he raced the Kieft-Norton on four more occasions. After a crash in May, in Brussels, the car was destroyed and although various "production" Kiefts were tried, none was as effective as the prototype. Moss pulled out of the Kieft deal and returned to Cooper, while retaining the Norton engine. He won two more races in 1952 and four in 1953, including a 5 lapper at the Nürburgring, equivalent to 114 kilometres.

On the Formula 2 front, he continued with HWM. John Heath and Alf Francis had built a new car; this time a true single seater with a tubular chassis and a De Dion rear axle. Moss tested it for the first time at Goodwood on 9th March 1951. He felt it had promise and noted in his log book. "It seems much better than last year's and I was able to take the second corner after the pits flat." The first race at Goodwood saw him beat Eric Brandon in the new Cooper 1100, with Lance Macklin fourth. Moss then went to Marseille and San Remo, where he finished fifth in a Formula 1 race dominated by the 4.5 litre Ferrari 375s driven by Ascari and Villoresi. The foreign races were much longer than the English sprints and the competition was stronger, both in terms of man and machine. On 13th May, the Monza Grand Prix was run over two legs with the classification decided by adding the times from both. Stirling fought with the Gordinis of Maurice Trintignant and Andre Simon in the first leg. He managed to close up to the back of Villoresi's Ferrari and it was then that Stirling first experienced the delights of slipstreaming. He immediately made the most of it. Slotting in behind the Ferrari – a 4.5 litre let us not forget! – he noticed that his 2 litre engine which usually peaked at 5400 rpm down the straight, would run all the way to 5900 rpm. The Ferrari was punching such a hole in the air that, even lifting off the throttle, Moss could stay in its slipstream. He finished the first leg right behind Villoresi in third place and maintained that position after the second. It was a very busy weekend. The very next day, the Monday of whitsun, Moss was back at Goodwood where he ran the brand new Kieft-Norton, winning the final and setting a new lap record, before returning to Italy. On 20th May, in Genoa, he was leading the Christopher Columbus Grand Prix in the HWM, when his transmission broke. A week later at Berne-Bremgarten, Moss took part in the Swiss Grand Prix, his first ever World Championship event. What could he hope for, driving a Formula 2 car up against the Ferrari 375 F1, Alfetta 159 and Talbot-Lago? In the pouring rain, Stirling and the HWM shone as the car's light weight and manoeuvrability suited the conditions. Tenacity also played a part as, towards half-distance, the screen broke, showering the driver's face with bits of broken glass. He drove thirty laps holding on to his visor with one hand and driving with the other. He was 7th when, at the end of the last lap, the Alta engine started spluttering as it ran out of fuel. Moss finished 8th and proved his determination.

● **22**_Berne, 27th May 1951: The very first of his 66 World Championship events, in a Formula 2 HWM, running with all the Formula 1 machinery. He finished 8th. Note the paved track surface at the Bremgarten circuit, making it dangerous in the wet.

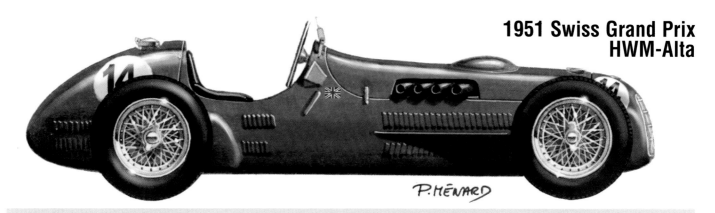

1951 Swiss Grand Prix
HWM-Alta

P. MÉNARD

Designers: John Heath and Alf Francis

Engine

Make/Type: Alta
Number of cylinders/configuration: 4 in line (front)
Capacity: 1960 cc
Bore x Stroke: 83.5 x 90 mm
Compression ratio: 10.5:1
Maximum power: 150 bhp
Maximum revs: 5800 rpm
Block material: light alloy
Carburettors: 2 Weber twin-bodied
Valve gear: twin overhead camshafts
Number of valves per cylinder: 2
Ignition: magneto

Transmission

Gearbox/number of gears: Armstrong Siddeley/4 pre-selector
Clutch: multi-plate

Chassis

Type: multitubular
Suspension: independent, helical springs (front); quarter-elliptical springs, de Dion rear axle (rear)
Dampers: Telescopic dampers
Wheels: 550 x 17 (front) / 600 x 17 (rear)
Tyres: Dunlop
Brakes: Wheel mounted drum brakes

Dimensions

Wheelbase: 2250 mm
Width: 1220 mm (front and rear)
Dry weight: 610 kg
Fuel capacity: 120 litres

Used in the 1951 Swiss Grand Prix and in around twenty non-championship events in 1951 and '52.

He would need it. Race meetings came in such rapid succession that the small teams, like HWM and Gordini, which needed to chase the start money, had neither time nor budget to overhaul their cars in between races. This meant there were frequent engine, gearbox and suspension failures, leading to frustrating retirements, as happened at Rouen and Avus for Moss. The race at Avus, the high speed circuit on the outskirts of Berlin, brought further annoying frustration. Not only did his engine break, trying to keep up with more powerful machinery down the two very long straights on the autobahn sections, but he also missed out on a golden opportunity. When he arrived in Berlin, Ken Gregory rang Moss to let him know Enzo Ferrari had sent a telegram offering him a drive in a works 375 F1 for the ACF and European Grand Prix! The only problem was that the event took place at Reims on the same day as the Avus event. Regrettably and out of respect for his HWM contract, Moss had to turn down the offer. Nevertheless, the day after a race at Erlen in Switzerland, before heading home for England,

Stirling pointed his humble Morris Minor in the direction of Maranello where he met Enzo Ferrari in person. He was made a fabulous offer, to drive for the factory team in 1952, starting with the Argentine Temporada race in January, where he would team up with Ascari and Villoresi. As preparation for this event, he would drive the new 4 cylinder 2.5 litre Ferrari in the Bari Grand Prix on 2nd September. Moss accepted with the proviso that *"John Heath has not entered the HWM."* The two men spoke in French, their only common language, even though neither of them mastered it very well. In the meantime, John Heath pulled out of Bari. But when Moss turned up for practice and sat in the cockpit of the Ferrari for the first time to check the driving position, he was told by a Scuderia mechanic that the car was reserved for Piero Taruffi. Was it a misunderstanding or a linguistic mix up? Or a deliberate ploy? Moss never found out, but from that day, he developed a bitter resentment towards Enzo Ferrari, which was only cleared up over the winter of 1961-62. During those ten years, he liked nothing better than to beat "those devilish red cars."

Stirling's other option to get into Formula 1 was all the more tempting as it was an English one. It was called BRM (British Racing Motors,) the company set up by the driver Raymond Mays and the engineer Peter Berthon, in Bourne, Lincolnshire. It was an impressive machine with a V 16, 1500 cc supercharged engine. It was slow and lacked finesse. Built in the former ERA workshops, as Berthon was one of the bosses there, it was financed by a group of industrial sponsors and thousands of British supporters who subscribed to the project. The directors lost a packet running the firm and through its public (and private) relations and spent a fortune hiring top line drivers like Fangio, while the car had several design faults. Moss first tried it at Folkingham aerodrome in July 1951, then had another go at Monza in October and again in Italy in February and March 1952. "*At first, it seemed like a major project,*" he admitted. "*I had to try it. Unfortunately, it was the worst car I have ever driven. The suspension was horrible with 30 centimetres of travel over the cobbled bumps at Monza! And the engine, although very powerful, had nothing below 10,000 rpm. It was undriveable. But I was not yet well known enough to tell them to their face. And also, I*

wasn't experienced enough to do much about it." Moss raced the BRM V16 just once, at the Dundrod Ulster Trophy in June 1952. It ended in retirement when the engine overheated. The only consolation on the day was to pass Fangio spinning the other BRM V16 going the other way!

In any case, the 1952 World Championship would be contested with Formula 2 cars, partly because the BRMs were not ready and kept pulling out and also because of the withdrawal of Alfa Romeo. Moss would race the HWM three more times, his best result a non-championship second place at the Eifel, behind the Ferrari of Swiss privateer Rudi Fischer. Then he turned his attentions to other projects, which yet again, would only flatter to deceive. First there was the "G" type ERA. It was his friend and Jaguar sports car driver Leslie Johnson who dragged him into this painful episode. Johnson bought the ERA (English Racing Automobiles) marque off Humphrey Cook, who with Peter Berthon was its co-founder. Before the war, they built some marvellous "Voiturettes" with 1500 cc supercharged engines. But the Formula 2 car was nowhere near the mark. It was designed by a Cambridge engineer, David Hodkin, built in Dunstable and used a Bristol 6 cylinder engine

● **23**_Dundrod, 7th June 1952: this rare photo shows two V16 BRMs on the first lap of the Ulster Trophy. While Moss tackles the hairpin, Fangio is approaching it backwards. Both cars retired, Moss' with a broken clutch.
(The Autocar Editorial)

• **24**_Silverstone, 19ᵗʰ July 1952: the British Grand Prix. Moss did what he could with the ERA Type G. He retired with an overheating engine.

fitted to a home made chassis with big tubular beams. To lower it, thus improving its road holding, the driving position was moved to the right, with the driveshaft passing to the left of the driver. Unfortunately, lack of funds saw the project fail. Moss appreciated the rigidity of the chassis, the brakes and first class steering, but in the Grands Prix, the car was not competitive. In Spa, the engine broke and seized on the first lap of the Belgian Grand Prix. Moss had only just got going when the ERA crashed into a milestone post. It was repaired in time for the British Grand Prix at Silverstone. In the race, the engine was overheating and Stirling spun, pushing too hard to make up for the drop in power. During this time, Mike Hawthorn started to make a name for himself, coming 4ᵗʰ and 3ʳᵈ in these two Grands Prix, at the wheel of a simple Cooper-Bristol behind the untouchable Ferraris. He joined the Ferrari squad for 1953, much to Moss' annoyance.

Towards the end of the season, the ERA "G" put up a few respectable performances, but Moss realised it was outclassed when it came to the Grands Prix. For the Italian Grand Prix at Monza, Moss chose to race a Connaught A type, a good car from the marque established by two industrialists with a love of racing; Rodney Clarke and Kenneth McAlpine. It had very strong magnesium wheels and good road holding, but the Lea Francis sports car engine lacked power, despite running fuel injection, something of a novelty at the time. The transporter carrying the three Connaughts for the race arrived in Milan the night before practice. Once unloaded, McAlpine, Dennis Poore and Moss drove them by road to the circuit, escorted in the dead of night by a Police motorcylist leading them at speeds in excess of 100 km/h! In the race, Moss retired with valve gear failure. He was back in a Connaught for the 1953 Dutch Grand Prix, finishing ninth.

• **25**_Monza, 7ᵗʰ September 1952: fed up with the ERA Type G, Moss switched to a works Type A Connaught. The engine broke while he was lying second.

Another English project, another fiasco: the Cooper-Alta. This new single-seater was built in a hurry over the winter of 1952-53, with the collaboration of Ray Martin, whom Moss trusted after the success of the Kieft 500. It was based on a John A. Cooper design. He was an Autocar journalist and engineer, not to be confused with John Cooper, son of Charles, even though these were the men who built the car in their Surbiton workshop. On paper, one of its strengths was its front disc brakes, a novelty on single-seaters, but the inboard rear drum brakes were a very bad idea, as oil from the De Dion rear axle leaked into the brake fluid. On top of that, the chassis lacked rigidity, while the front end and other components were fragile and badly designed. The first outing at Goodwood in 1953 at Easter turned to farce. At the Eifel, Moss finished sixth, which was a major achievement. At the ACF Grand Prix at Reims, the flywheel broke and bits came shooting out between the driver's legs! The race was won by Hawthorn's Ferrari, beating Fangio in the Maserati. Moss and Alf Francis decided to quickly buy a standard Cooper Mark II. Francis and his assistant, Tony Robinson modified it in the Cooper workshops in Surbiton, fitting the Alta engine with its "HWM-style" pre-selector gearbox. It took them just eleven days to build the car! Running on a nitro-methane mixture, it put out 200 horsepower. It powered Stirling to sixth in the German Grand Prix, but in those days there were no points for sixth place. The "Cooper-Alta Mk II" finished 13th in Italy, having run fifth for much of the time until the tyres gave up under the fast pace. It also scored some fine results in English races (Crystal Palace, Prescott and Goodwood) but returned a blank score sheet in the 1953 World Championship. In 1954, patriotism would have to be put to one side and a foreign car would be needed. ■

• **26**_Monza, 19th September 1953: in the 1953 Italian Grand Prix, the Cooper-Alta Mk II was going like a rocket, thanks to a nitromethane fuel mix. Moss finished 13th after a hellish race with his tyres worn down to the canvas.

• **27**_Crystal Palace, 16th September 1953: a win for Moss and the Cooper-Alta in the London Trophy, run over two legs.
(The Autocar Editorial)

Chapter 6
1954
In the points at last!

• **28**_Spa-Francorchamps, 20th June 1954: Stirling's first points and first podium in the World Championship. He finished 3rd in his own Maserati 250 F in the Belgian Grand Prix, behind Fangio's works Maserati 250 F and Trintignant in a works Ferrari 625.

My father and my manager Ken Gregory
went to see Alfred Neubauer on my
behalf, because we knew that at the end
of 1953, Mercedes was preparing for a big racing
comeback. Neubauer told them that he had yet
to see me race in a competitive car, that they
should try and find me one and then he would
see. That's why they went to Maserati, who were
happy to sell them a 250 F, at a cost of 3,500,000
lire. It was the only way of getting a worthwhile
Formula 1 car, as Ferrari did not sell any and over
here, the Vanwall did not exist yet."

Stirling was finally going to get his hands
on a real Grand Prix machine, just as the new 2.5
litre Formula 1 was coming into force. He was
impatient to show what he could do. The hors
d'oeuvre to his 1954 season was the Monte Carlo
Rally in January, at the wheel of a Sunbeam-
Talbot 90, with John A. Cooper and Desmond
Scannell. It was his third Monte, always with the
same co-drivers and always with the same works
car from the Rootes group. Second, 4 seconds
behind the winner in 1952 was a good debut.
They finished sixth in 1953, but this time only
fifteenth. Stirling drove all the timed sections. He
would do better still in the Alpine Rally.

While waiting for the start of the Grand
Prix season, he accepted an offer from the rich
American team owner, Briggs Cunningham, to
drive in the Sebring 12 Hours in March, where
Jaguar was not entered. Moss would drive a small

open car, the Osca MT with a 1500 cc engine,
with Bill Lloyd, Cunningham's son-in-law as co-
driver. He really enjoyed himself, taking an
unexpected win, which to cap it all, was his first
in an event which counted towards the
Constructors' World Championship for sports cars,
established in 1953. Their task was definitely
made easier by the many mechanical failures –
broken gearboxes and rear axles especially –
which lap after lap on this very tough and bumpy
track, eliminated or delayed the favourites, such
as the privately entered Ferrari 4.5 litre,
Cunningham, Aston Martin and especially the
factory Lancias. The little Osca was not spared, as
it finished the race with absolutely no brakes at
all. Moss had driven the last stint, using the
gearbox and taking different lines into the
corners to compensate for the problem.

It was while travelling back to New York, to
take the Queen Mary home to England that the
driver learnt that an order had been placed in
Modena for a Maserati. It was chassis 2508. Alf
Francis and Tony Robinson would look after it.
The Rootes group would lend a Commer van to
carry the tyres, spares and tools and to tow the
trailer. In April, while Stirling was racing at Oulton
Park and Goodwood in Sports Cars and Formula 3,
Alf went to Modena to help prepare the car,
which was running late. He spoke to engineer
Guerrino Bertocchi about modifications Moss had
asked for: an accelerator pedal on the right, as

used on road cars (the one on the first 250 F was in the middle of the pedal box like pre-war race cars,) and a longer driving position than standard.

Finally, on 5th May, accompanied by Tony Robinson, Stirling arrived at the local race track in Modena, around 100 kilometres to the south of Milan. The car was run-in on the track by Alf and Bertocchi. In the morning, Moss had his first drive in the car and noted in his journal: "*Track covered in oil as our tank was over filled. A marvellous feeling from the car. I did around fifteen laps, nudging 7000 rpm in fifth and 6500 in the lower gears. My time, 1'4'2. We all had lunch and then set off. John drove me and Pat to Milan where we stopped off at the Palace. Had a good meal at the Napoli then went to a jazz club. In bed at 2.30*" F1 drivers knew how to live in those days!

His first race with "2508," painted British Racing Green, was at Bordeaux on 9th May. In practice in the wet, Stirling found the car, fitted with Dunlops, heavy to drive. It was raining for the race and Alf fitted Pirellis, which transformed its handling. On this rather slow street circuit, Moss finished 4th, the sole surviving Maserati behind the Ferraris of Gonzalez, Manzon and Trintignant. A week later at Silverstone, the International Trophy was run over two legs. Moss finished third in the first one. In the second, he tried not to go past the 7200 rpm mark to conserve the engine, As things turned out it was the De Dion axle which let him down! At Aintree, on 29th May in a 200 mile race, he scored a sparkling success, coming third in his heat and won the final with a 48 second lead over second

● **30**_Bordeaux, 9th May 1954: this non-championship race on a street circuit attracted a high class entry. For his very first race in the Maserati 250 F chassis 2508, fresh from the Modena workshops, Moss finished fourth behind the Ferraris of Gonzalez, Manzon and Trintignant.
(Photo Bernard Cahier)

● **31**_Silverstone, 15th May 1954: with this Jaguar Mk VII, which he was keen on, Moss had to settle for 3rd in the BRDC Production race. He was on pole, but the starter motor jammed at the moment he tried to get away and he had to rock the heavy saloon back and forth several times to get it going!

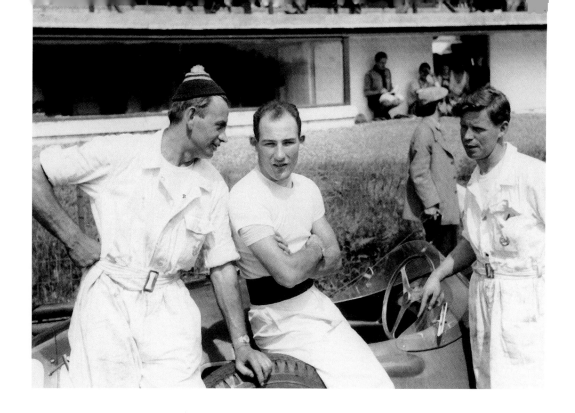

• **32**_Aintree, 29th May 1954: before the start of the Aintree 20, which marked his first win in the Maserati 250 F, Moss chats with Alf Francis (on left) and his assistant Tony Robinson.

• **33**_Spa-Francorchamps, 20th June 1954: this magnificent view of the legendary 14.5 km Ardennes road circuit shows Moss attacking Eau Rouge in the Belgian Grand Prix. Today, the circuit measures just 6.940 km, but it still has plenty of character.

placed Reg Parnell. The mechanics had changed the injectors, transforming the car's performance. In the Rome Grand Prix, Moss fought for the lead with the works 250 F of young Argentine, Onofre Marimon, who was a protégé of Fangio. A gear on the De Dion broke and Bertocchi promised Moss stronger ones for the Belgian Grand Prix at Spa on 20th June. The new parts would only turn up on Saturday, the eve of the race and Alf and Tony repaired the transmission in time for qualifying.

At the end of the first session, Moss was a bit depressed to have done no better than 4'46", although he improved to 4'40"8 the next day, thanks to Bertocchi's advice to fit new Pirelli tyres. Fangio was on pole in 4'22"11! Alf Francis

then discovered that Fangio's works 250 F was running to 8100 rpm, 900 rpm more than Moss' customer car, which was some consolation for the Englishman. Fangio won the race after a frantic dice with the Ferraris of Farina, Hawthorn and Trintignant. The Frenchman came second with Moss third, finally scoring his first points in the world championship. Sadly, they would be the only ones of the year. He was unable to take part in the ACF Grand Prix at Reims, as Maserati asked him to do them a rather unusual favour. Fangio had just left Maserati, as planned, to join Mercedes who were due to debut the W 196 at this race. Therefore the trident marque wanted to line up Ascari and Villoresi, loaned by Lancia while

1954 Belgian Grand Prix (Team Moss) Maserati 250 F

P. MÉNARD

Designers: Gioacchino Colombo and Giulio Alfieri

Engine
Make/Type: Maserati 250 F
Number of cylinders/configuration: 6 in line (front)
Capacity: 2493.9 cc
Bore x stroke: 84 x 75 mm
Compression ratio: 12:1
Maximum power: 240 horsepower
Maximum revs: 7000 rpm
Block material: light alloy
Carburettors: 3 Weber twin-bodied
Valve gear: twin overheads camshafts
Number of valves per cylinder: 2
Ignition: 2 magnetos (Marelli)
Number of spark plugs per cylinder: 2

Transmission
Gearbox/number of gears: transverse Maserati (5)
Clutch: Maserati

Chassis
Type: tubular
Suspension: independent (front); de Dion rear axle (rear)
Dampers: Hydraulic dampers, transverse leaf springs at rear.
Wheels: 5.50 x 16 (front) / 700 x 16 (rear)
Tyres: Pirelli
Brakes: Wheel mounted drum brakes

Dimensions
Wheelbase: 2250 mm
Width: 1300 mm (front) / 1240 mm (rear)
Dry weight: 620 kg

Used in Belgium and Spain in 1954 and fifteen non-championship race's in 1954 and '55.

waiting for their D 50 to be ready, to squire Marimon. But there was a shortage of 250 Fs (unlike today when historic races often feature more of them than were ever built originally.) So the factory asked Moss to "lend" his 250 F to Villoresi. "Gigi" made good use of it, coming 5th, but Moss, who was at the race as a spectator, derived some benefit from the deal. His car was taken to Modena and completely rebuilt to the latest factory specification: rear mounted oil tank, a new head and shorter ratio first gear. Better still, Maserati guaranteed to repair Moss' engine free of charge if it broke. Right from the next race, the British Grand Prix at Silverstone on 17th July, Stirling ventured up the rev range to 7800 rpm. He started on the front row alongside the

• **34**_Nürburgring, 1st August 1954: opening lap of the German Grand Prix as Moss makes his debut as a works driver, but at the wheel of his own 250 F! Fangio (Mercedes) chases Gonzalez (Ferrari) and pulls away from Moss (Maserati) who is fighting off the Mercedes of Kling and Herrmann.

• **35**_Monza, 5th September 1954: the Italian Grand Prix saw a great battle between Moss (Maserati) and Ascari (Ferrari.) Alberto went out on lap 49 with a broken valve and Fangio won in a Mercedes that was not in the best of health.
(The Aurtocar Editorial)

• **36**_In this Italian Grand Prix, Moss had to stop on lap 68 of 80 to top up the Maserati with oil. Then a pipe broke. He finished the race dying of thirst, having pushed the 250 F to finish tenth!
(The Aurtocar Editorial)

Ferrari's of Gonzalez and Hawthorn and Fangio's Mercedes. He spent much of the race in second place behind Gonzalez and ahead of Fangio. It was not be and the Maserati's transmission let go on lap 80 of 90. At a non-championship race at Caen, Moss finished second to Trintignant's Ferrari. Then, on the eve of the German Grand Prix, Maserati offered him a works drive. "2508" was repainted in red, apart from the nose which remained green. Marimon gave Stirling a warm welcome to the team. Tragically, perhaps destabilised by the arrival of such a strong team-mate, he tried too hard, going off the road in practice, killing himself. The Maserati mechanics were distraught, but did their best to prepare Moss' car, but he retired yet again, this time on the second lap. This time it was a con-rod. He failed to finish any further grands prix. In Berne he retired and again in Monza, where he stopped with an oil leak while leading the Italian Grand Prix from Fangio's Mercedes and then failed to finish in Spain. Many of the retirements were

caused when oil lines broke because they had not been sufficiently protected from engine vibrations. But at least, Moss had done enough to impress Alfred Neubauer, who had made note of the young man's progress.

Apart from a podium finish in Spa and wins in non-championship events at Aintree and Goodwood, 1954 was a frustrating season for Moss on several levels. The same applied to endurance racing, as the new Jaguar D type, entrusted to him by the Coventry factory and quicker than the C, retired in the Le Mans 24 Hours (brakes) and the Reims 12 Hours (transmission.) In the Tourist Trophy in Dundrod, his third and last race in a D type ended in a lowly 18th place, as the engine was losing oil pressure. It comes as no surprise therefore that he never placed the glorious Jaguar D type very high in the pantheon of cars he had driven.

• **37**_Oulton Park, 13ᵗʰ August 1954: Stirling in his Maserati, attacks Parnell's Ferrari on his way to winning the Gold Cup. *(The Aurtocar Editorial)*

● **38**_Dundrod,
14th September 1954: Moss
shared the works Jaguar D type
with Peter Walker and only
finished 18th in the Tourist
Trophy as a drop in oil pressure
forced Stirling yet again to
push the car to the flag.
(The Aurtocar Editorial)

Strangely enough, apart from Formula 3, in
which he contested one final season with a
Beart-Cooper Mk VII (10 races, 6 wins,) it was in
rallying that Moss would make his mark that year.
Today, it is unthinkable that a Schumacher or a
Coulthard or a Montoya would compete in the
Acropolis or San Remo Rally in between two F1
Grands Prix and what is more, would win them!
But that is exactly what Moss did in the Coupe
des Alpes in 1952, '53 and '54. It was run in July
over 4000 kilometres of very tough roads,
comprising an incredible number of mountain
climbs in France, Switzerland, Austria and Italy,
running through the night. Along with the
famous Liege-Rome-Liege it was the absolute
pinnacle of road events for both man and
machine. The very best touring and grand touring
cars took part as did specialist drivers like
Belgium's Johnny Claes and Englishman Ian
Appleyard, who, co-driven by his wife, had
already won it three years running in his Jaguar

XK 120, without picking up any penalty points.
This feat had earned him a "Coupe d'Or des
Alpes," the only man to win one. After the 1952
Monte Carlo Rally, the Rootes competitions
manager, Norman Garrad entrusted Moss and
expert co-driver John Cutts with a Sunbeam
Talbot 90 for the Alpine Rally. Another one was
entered for Mike Hawthorn. *"We were both paid
50 pounds sterling to do the rally. Imagine that
today!"* remarked Stirling. At the finish, there
were ten cars with no penalties, of which three of
the five works Sunbeams, including the Moss-
Cutts car. After effecting repairs to an exhaust
pipe cost them 26 minutes, Stirling had to drive
every leg flat out in order not to drop time at the
controls. The Sunbeams were classified eighth,
ninth and tenth, winning a Coupe des Alpes for
the team. In 1953, the Rootes group launched the
Sunbeam Alpine convertible and was promoting
the car with a series of records at Jabbeke in
Belgium and at Montlhery. Moss took part

naturally. Then he was immediately back with John Cutts, for the Alpine Rally which took place between the ACF and the British Grands Prix. Apart from a few problems at the start of the route, including losing a rally plate on the road, Moss and Cutts again had a penalty-free run, picking up a second Coupe des Alpes.

For the third attempt in 1954, again in a Sunbeam Alpine, Moss and Cutts pulled off the hat-trick. That July there was still snow in the Alps, so that it seemed more like January. It allowed them to save tyres, Stirling noted philosophically. But in the car, the two men were freezing. The last leg was exhausting as it went from Cortina d'Ampezzo to Cannes, via the Dolomites, then the cols of Stelvio, the little Saint-Bernard, Iseran, Croix-de-Fer, Galibier and Cayolle. Twenty nine hours on the road, during which Moss gave his all to escape the penalties. The descent of the Cayolle down to Grasse left him gasping. When he arrived in Cannes and the

tension finally slipped away, he burst into tears. "Most extraordinary" he would note in his journal, admitting that for once he had lost his cool. Sheila Van Damm in the other Sunbeam Alpine made it too, despite going off the road. The Coupe d'Or was within their grasp. But there was still one more check to go. A scrutineer boarded the car to ride as a passenger to check that everything was working as it had at the start. Punished on the cols, the Sunbeam had lost 1st and 4th gear. That left just 2nd and 3rd and overdrive. Stirling pretended to select a gear with the lever, located under the steering wheel and unnoticed by the scrutineer, he engaged the overdrive. The scrutineer got out of the car with a "Congratulations Mr. Moss," which meant the much prized Coupe d'Or was his. Years later, Stirling confessed: "*It is the only time I cheated to get a win, but I reckon I bloody deserved that one.*" Who today would dare to disagree? ∎

• **39**_Moss and John Cutts in a convertible Sunbeam Alpine in July 1953 in the second of the three Alpine Rallies which they would dispute together, with penalty-free runs which earned them a Coupe d'Or. *(The Aurtocar Editorial)*

Chapter 7
1955 In Fangio's footsteps

● **40-41**_Aintree, 16th July 1955: glory days! Moss in Mercedes no. 12 takes his very first World Championship win ahead of Fangio (Mercedes no. 10.) Small photo: the victor's laurels for Moss and whispered words with Fangio.

• **42**_Hockenheim,
3rd December 1954: a private
test session with the
Mercedes W 196, which Moss
insisted on before signing the
contract. Note the curious
grilles never used in races.
(The Autocar Editorial)

It was in November 1954, while in New York and about to tackle the "Mountain Rally" in a Sunbeam that Moss heard from Ken Gregory, phoning from London that Mercedes was taking him on to tackle the 1955 season in Formula 1 and sports cars! "*It was so fantastic I couldn't get to sleep that night, just thinking about it,*" commented Stirling. As soon as the rally was over, he flew to Cologne to join his father and Ken. All three of them had a meeting on 4th December at Hockenheim to test the Mercedes W 196, as requested by Moss prior to signing the contract. Worth noting that this time, it was not Alfred Neubauer asking to test the driver. It was cold and damp and Moss learnt the circuit at the wheel of a 220 saloon. On a wet track, he lapped in 2'35." Finally, he jumped into the cockpit of the Formula 1 car. It was the most sought after machine of its day, with a powerful engine but less impressive handling. He found it heavy to drive and the brakes were wooden. He also had trouble adapting to the reverse pattern gearchange. Nevertheless, he gradually picked up the pace, managing to equal the best time set by Karl Kling that same day, in 2'15." Moss recalls being more impressed with the way the team was run than with the car. "*When I stopped, I had*

black grime over my face, thrown up by the brakes. Seeing me looking around for something to wipe myself down with, a mechanic rushed forward with a face cloth, a clean towel, soap and a bowl of water. But even more surprising, it was HOT water! In this place in the middle of nowhere I could tell I was dealing with people who believed in attention to detail."

It was obvious that Neubauer, whom Moss revered, was counting more on him than on Kling and Herrmann to back up Fangio and counter the Lancia menace in the 1955 World Championship. Moss does not speak German, but he established a rapport with the engineer, Rudolf Uhlenhaut, who had an English mother and spoke perfect English. A bit later, Stirling and his father met with Neubauer to sign the contract. The document had been prepared by Ken Gregory during a previous meeting at Mercedes and included a clause stating that start and prize money would be divided as follows: 10% for the mechanics and the remaining 90% divided equally between the driver and the constructor, which was standard practice back then. On top of that and less common, was an additional payment on signature of the contract. Moss got a thousand pounds sterling, which was less than Fangio, but the two

men shared the privilege of being allowed to race for other marques in Formula 1 or sports cars, at races where Mercedes was not entered. A further clause stated the drivers got a Mercedes road car as a perk of the job, to travel between races. Fangio got a 300 limousine, while Moss and the others had to make do with a 220.

The 1955 World Championship got underway on 16th January with the Argentine Grand Prix in Buenos Aires, held at the "17th October" circuit. It was a stifling hot day and local hero Fangio was one of the few not to suffer in the conditions. He was at the wheel of a short wheelbase W196, as was Karl Kling. According to Moss, Fangio's win proved the man's "superhuman" abilities. Stirling and Hans

Herrmann ran 1954 long wheelbase W 196s. Starting from third on the grid, the Englishman chased Fangio and Gonzalez's Ferrari, in close company with Ascari (Lancia D 50) and Farina (Ferrari.) His rivals were forced to stop, destroyed by the heat, so Moss found himself second behind the immovable Fangio, when on lap 30 the engine packed up because of a vapour lock in the injection system. Moss got out of the car and assuming he was exhausted, marshals plonked him on a stretcher and headed for the hospital! Luckily, an interpreter was found and the Englishman was "set free." He ran back to the pits, getting behind the wheel of Herrmann's car, which had already been taken over by Kling, whom he helped to fourth place.

• **45**_Buenos Aires,
30th January 1955: the Buenos
Aires Grand Prix was run as a
Formula Libre race in two legs.
Third in the first one, Moss
won the second in this
Mercedes W 196 with a 3 litre
engine (a prototype for the
300 SLR Sport.)
(The Autocar Editorial)

Two weeks later, the Mercedes team competed in the Buenos Aires Grand Prix, on a modified version of the same track. It was run as a Formula Libre event, outside the World Championship. It provided Mercedes with the opportunity of trying the new 3 litre engine, which would be fitted to the 300 SLR sports car. Fangio, Moss and Kling ran long wheelbase 1954 cars, with air ducts and deflectors above the front wheels to shield the drivers from the heat and brake dust. It rained heavily in qualifying, but it was once again torrid during the race. The Continental tyres lacked grip and Nino Farina, driving a Pirelli-shod Ferrari 3 litre won the first heat. But the 1950 World Champion succumbed to nerves and spun at the start of the second

heat and, demoralised, handed over the car to Gonzalez, who restarted one lap down on the two Mercedes. At that moment, Maurice Trintignant in the other Ferrari was chasing the Mercedes. He was getting dangerously close as the finish drew near. Moss, who was following Fangio, had no option but to overtake the Argentine, to contain the Frenchman. He won the leg (89th win from 250 races) but Fangio took the Grand Prix when the times for both legs were added up.

Moss went back to the United States to race in the Sebring 12 Hours on 13th March. This time, it was Lance Macklin, his old friend from HWM, who offered him a drive. Lance had just bought an Austin Healey 100 S, a 4 cylinder, 2.6 litre machine, which he had driven from

• **46**_Moss with Lance
Macklin in the Austin Healey
100 S for the Dr. Sebring
12 Hours.

New York to Florida! The car was not very powerful (140 horsepower) but it was strong. Stirling made a demon start, as only he could. He ran flat out for the car, jumped over the door and led the pack. He told us his secret. *"When I was sixteen, I could run the 100 metres in 10 seconds, which isn't bad. But later, I learnt a technique for the "Le Mans" type starts with the Jaguar C type. At first, I left the door open but then I decided it was better to leave the door shut and jump over it, with the car already in first gear. So I would land with my left foot on the clutch and my hand on the ignition. It was worth a fraction of a second and meant one got away from the pack in case there was an accident in the middle of it."* At Sebring, Moss and Macklin finished sixth overall, behind a D type, two Ferraris and two Maseratis and won their class. Lance Macklin entered the same Austin Healey 100 S in the Le Mans 24 Hours, an event which would be hit by tragedy.

In between non-championship races at Goodwood and Bordeaux in April, when he was reunited with his good old Maserati 250 F, Stirling put in a lot of time training at the Hockenheim track and on Italian roads, in preparation for the Mille Miglia. It was the first race of the season with the brand new Mercedes 300 SLR. It was also one of the toughest. The Stuttgart firm was desperate to win and had invested heavily in the event, with three months of preparation and practice, four cars entered and they recced the 1600 kilometres route from Brescia to Rome and back again. The drivers and co-drivers practised the route in 220 saloons, then with 300 SL coupes and finally with 300 SLR "T" cars. Moss remembered covering the most difficult sections at race speed, to test the equipment. Finally, one month before "D" day, the four race 300 SLRs were tested at Hockenheim by their respective drivers: chassis 0003 for Fangio (who would drive alone,) 0004 for Moss, partnered by journalist Denis Jenkinson, 0005 for Kling (like Fangio driving alone) and 0006 for Herrmann with the mechanic Hermann Eger.)

The Mille Miglia is a legendary event, a mad race which millions of Italians turned out to watch every year since 1927, with the exception of the war years and which ran until 1957. On closed roads, it was like a non-stop rally special stage with all the danger implied therein, mainly because of the massive crowds along almost its entire length, especially when the route went through towns and villages. On top of that, between 500 and 600 cars started at minute intervals from Brescia, the smallest first, so that the drivers of the more powerful cars faced a continuous stream of overtaking moves. The most powerful? Ferrari, Maserati, Mercedes, open Formula Sport cars just like those which competed in the Le Mans 24 Hours or the Sebring 12 Hours on closed circuits, capable of hitting speeds in excess of 280 km/h. Up to now, Moss had always been unlucky on the Mille Miglia (see chapter 5.) It was impossible to memorise such a long and complex route with thousands of corners, hard obstacles, houses, hump-back bridges and level crossings. So Moss brought along Denis Jenkinson, who would write a legendary report of the race in Motor Sport magazine. In 1949, "Jenks" had passengered Eric Oliver, the sidecar world champion. Proof enough that behind his horn-rimmed glasses and his long red beard, he was not a man who scared easily. Moss was particularly impressed by his extremely ingenious system of notes, fitted on a roll of paper under a perspex cover. As helmets with radios were not yet invented, the two men set up a sign language to understand one another above the cacophany of the Mercedes 8 cylinder engine and the wind noise. There was one further element to this meticulous preparation. Fangio gave both men a pill each to combat fatigue. Stirling took his before the start, Jenkinson pocketed his, which Alfred Moss later had analysed in a laboratory. They set off on 1st May at 7h22 on board the "722," leaving the famous start ramp in Brescia. They hoped to finish third behind Fangio and Kling to contribute to a Mercedes triumph. They found themselves in the lead at the Rome time control. The driver picks up the story: *"On the first straight section leading to Verona, the SLR was running at 7500 rpm in 5th, equivalent to around 280 km/h, but we were caught by Castellotti, who had started after us in his big 4.4 litre 6 cylinder Ferrari. I was pushing on but without taking any real risks, keeping the wheels away from the verges and pavements. But coming into Padua at 240 km/h, I braked too late for a 90 degree right at the end of the main street. I went straight on for as long as I dared, then I let go of the brakes and I had to let the front end go into a slide. The front left wing hit the straw bales, the car bounced back in the right*

*direction and I accelerated again, cursing my
carelessness and keeping an eye on the gauges to
see if the engine temperature was going to climb,
or the oil pressure drop."*

But none of that happened as the 300 SLR
seemed remarkably robust. Castellotti seized the
moment to get past. They followed him closely to
Ravenna, which was enough to show them he
was trying too hard. Sure enough, the Ferrari
soon had to stop for a tyre change. Near Pescara,
down a straight, "Jenks" indicated they were
approaching a bump to be taken at 7500 rpm in
5ᵗʰ, or 280 km/h. Stirling obeyed the instruction,
but felt the car was airborne for rather a long
time. It was a relief when it landed with the
wheels pointing straight ahead. With all the
movement, Jenkinson had to lean out of the car
to be sick and lost his glasses. Luckily he had
thought to bring along a spare pair. They had the
time card stamped at Pescara and stopped at the
Mercedes service area. A swarm of mechanics fell
on the car, throwing in 80 litres of fuel, just
enough to get to Rome, fitting four wheels with
new tyres, cleaning the windscreen, handing Moss
and his co-driver a peeled banana and a quarter
of an orange. They were shown a note: "Taruffi,
Moss 15 seconds, Herrmann, Kling, Fangio." The
driver was worried while covering the last ten
kilometres into Rome, as walls of spectators along
the route forced him to slow to 210 km/h instead
of the planned 240 km/h. At Rome, just over half-
distance (874 kilometres covered to be precise,)
Moss cut the engine for the one and only time in
the whole race and jumped from the Mercedes to
deal with a pressing need! The 50 second stop

was enough to refuel and Jenkinson was handed
another note: they had passed Taruffi! Moss was
sceptical, as an old Mille Miglia proverb goes:
*"whoever is in the lead in Rome, is never at the
finish in Brescia."*

They would make a lie of that proverb.
Jenkinson made one mistake in the notes, when
an over-filled fuel tank splashed petrol on his
neck. They spun once on the pass Radicofani
because of badly adjusted front brakes and Moss
saved the situation with a frantic reversing move.
They beat the record for the Florence to Bologna
stage, which included the passes of Futa and
Raticosa. They were the first to arrive in Brescia,
having covered the 1597 km in 10 hours,
7 minutes and 48 seconds, at an average speed of
157.650 km/h. The record would never be beaten.
On Sunday night, after a good bath, the prize-
giving ceremony and a dinner, Moss found it
impossible to get to sleep. At a quarter past
midnight, he got up, got dressed, packed his bags
and got behind the wheel of his Mercedes 220
saloon. He drove alone through the night to
Stuttgart. The next day, he lunched with the
Mercedes directors and then took the plane to
London. *"Fangio's little pills really worked well,"*
he noted in his journal.

After an interlude at Silverstone in his old
Maserati 250 F, Moss was back with the Mercedes
team for the Monaco Grand Prix, on 22ⁿᵈ May. In
qualifying, an on-form Ascari slipped his Lancia
D 50 between Fangio on pole and Moss in the
other Mercedes. Fangio was leading when
unusually the Mercedes engine broke down. A
surprised Moss, who had been following him thus

took the lead. Then on lap 81 of 100, his engine also expired! This left Ascari in the lead, but not for long as his car careered off into the harbour as he was being chased by Trintignant's Ferrari. The Frenchman went on to win the race from Castelloti's Lancia. Stirling waited until the leader was on his very last lap, to push his car across the line to be classified ninth and last.

The Eifel Cup was held on 29th May for Formula Sport cars at the Nürburgring. Fangio won again from Moss, who noted that after the Mille Miglia the engine from his winning 300 SLR was put on a Mercedes race department test bed and delivered 296 horsepower at 7400 rpm, just as it had done before the start. The Stuttgart engineers definitely knew their stuff.

The days following these three magnificent races were some of the blackest in the sport's history. First of all, three days after diving into the waters at Monaco, Alberto Ascari was killed at Monza at the wheel of a Ferrari Sport car. It was a troubled time for all the Italians, who venerated him, the other drivers who respected him and for Gianni Lancia, whose team and company were on the verge of bankruptcy. Nevertheless, Eugenio Castellotti persuaded Gianni Lancia to let him race a D 50 in the Belgian Grand Prix on 5th June. The young Italian, in what was seen as a homage to Alberto, managed to take pole ahead of the Mercedes and even led the race before breaking down. From then on, it was back to normal with the Mercedes "train" heading the pack, Fangio winning from Moss yet again.

Then, on 11th June came catastrophe at the Le Mans 24 Hours. The tale has been told many

● **48**_Monaco, 22nd May 1955: after Fangio retires, Moss leads the Grand Prix, but on lap 81 of 100 his Mercedes suffers the same valve failure as the Argentine's and Maurice Trintignant wins for Ferrari. Moss, a dab hand at the procedure, pushed his car across the line to finish 10th.

● **49**_Nürburgring, 29th May 1955: the delight and friendship between Moss and Fangio is evident at the end of the Eifel Cup where they scored another Mercedes one-two in Formula Sport, with the 300 SLR.

● **50**_Spa-Francorchamps, 5th June 1955: Stirling Moss concentrates hard at the wheel of the Mercedes W 196 in the Belgian Grand Prix. He finished second to Fangio.

● **51**_Zandvoort, 19th June 1955: the Mercedes "train," Fangio ahead of Moss, on their way to a W 196 one-two in the Dutch Grand Prix, ahead of Italian coming-man, Luigi Musso.

times before (1.) Let us precise the events remembering what a popular race this was at the time, run in front of a crowd of 200,000 people around the 13.492 km circuit. Even back then, much of it was shown live on France's only television channel. Among the Formula 1 stars of the day who were taking part, driving for the top factory teams, Moss shared with Fangio one of the three 300 SLRs entered by the factory, fitted with a rear wind-break, operated hydraulically, which would give Moss his first experience of ground effect. At the start of the race, the Mercedes fought with the Ferraris and Jaguars, including Mike Hawthorn's D type. It was a last minute stop by Hawthorn which triggered the terrible accident, as his car fishtailed and braked heavily to make it into the pits. He was being followed closely by Macklin, in the Austin Healey used at the Sebring 12 Hours, who had to swerve to the left to stop running into the Jaguar. It was then that Levegh in the Mercedes, which was about to pass him, took off and exploded in the crowd, killing him and around 80 spectators, injuring several more.

(1)_*"Fangio"* in *"Formula 1 Legends"* collection.

Fangio, who had been following, saw a warning hand signal from Levegh and just managed to squeeze by. Despite the devastation, the race continued at the insistence of its director, Charles Faroux, who refused to give in to panic and immediately understood it was the best way to keep clear the access roads for the emergency vehicles. The telephone lines in the Le Mans area were jammed and it took Alfred Neubauer hours to finally get in touch with the Daimler-Benz bosses. Around half past midnight, the order came through from Germany: "out of respect for the victims" the two remaining Mercedes would pull out of the race, which included the Fangio-Moss car, then leading by a long way from the Hawthorn-Bueb Jaguar. To this day, Moss is not frightened of saying he did not agree with the decision, declaring it to be vain and theatrical. *"It was the same as admitting that it was Mercedes' fault, which it was not."* The Le Mans 24 Hours finished in the rain, with a meaningless win for the Hawthorn-Bueb Jaguar D type.

Designer: Rudolf Uhlenhaut

Engine

Make/type: Mercedes
Number of cylinders/configuration: 8 in line (front)
Capacity: 2496 cc
Bore x stroke: 76 x 68.8 mm
Compression ratio: 12.5:1
Maximum power: 290 horsepower
Maximum revs: 8500 rpm
Block material: steel
Fuel supply: Bosch direct injection
Valve gear: twin overhead camshafts
Number of valves per cylinder: 2 (desmodromic)
Ignition: magneto (Bosch)
Number of spark plugs per cylinder: 2
Weight: 204 kg

Transmission

Gearbox/number of gears: Mercedes box (5, 4 with synchro)
Clutch: dry, single plate

Chassis

Type: tubular
Suspensions: double wishbone, torsion bars, front anti-roll bar/ oscillating double-axle with lowered pivot point, rear torsion bar.
Dampers: telescopic dampers (front and rear)
Wheels: 600 x 16 (front) / 700 x 16 (rear)
Tyres: Continental
Freins: suspended drum brakes (ATE)

Dimensions

Wheelbase: 2200 mm/2130 mm/2350 mm (according to track)
Width: 1330 mm (front) / 1358 mm (rear)
Dry weight: 720 kg
Fuel capacity: 200 litres

Used from Argentina to Italy.

The furore kicked up by the accident, the most serious in the history of the sport, created a political storm, stirred up in the French press, which led to the banning of all racing in France up to the end of 1955, starting with the ACF Grand Prix, as well as those in Germany and Switzerland. However, the Dutch Grand Prix at Zandvoort on 19th June, just eight days after Le Mans, went ahead. There, another fiery young Italian, Luigi Musso in a Maserati, overtook Moss at the start. Stirling had a problem with his gear change gate, but he soon retook Musso and caught up with Fangio. "The train" was running again and the finish saw yet another Mercedes one-two, with Fangio ahead, thus increasing his lead over Moss in the World Championship.

"Neubauer didn't need to have a race strategy. He knew we had the best cars in the field," underlined Moss, when he answered our questions in Monaco in 2002. He went on to explain: *"he let us fight it out as we wished, right up to the moment when a Mercedes, it didn't*

matter which one, had a lead of 30 seconds. At that point he would hold out a board with "REG" on it, meaning "REGULAR" and the positions then had to remain unchanged." On 16th July, the British Grand Prix was run for the first time at Aintree, near Liverpool, better known for its horse racing track. Four Mercedes were lined up at the start: Moss on pole, Fangio at 2/10ths, with Kling and Taruffi on the second row. Behra had slipped his Maserati ahead of them on the front row. Fangio, Moss and Taruffi had a short wheelbase "Monaco" version fitted with external drum brakes with two other innovations: a rear anti-roll bar, adjustable from the cockpit, so the driver could alter the settings as the fuel load got lighter, thus altering the handling of the car and a screw mechanism on the gear change to prevent the driver selecting the wrong gear. Stirling takes up the story: *"Without any formal discussion or any team orders, I followed Fangio for quite a while before going ahead, Juan following me for a change. I am confident that, if* he had wanted to, he could have reversed the *order, but I was sure I would have made it difficult for him, because here I was, at last leading my Grand Prix."*

Moss made the most of overtaking a backmarker to pull out a slight lead over Fangio. On lap 50, he was leading his number one by 12 seconds. Neubauer then hung out the pitboard with the message "PI," "piano" in Italian and so the positions remained unchanged. All the same, Moss beat the lap record on lap 88 of 90, but Fangio closed up and on lap 89, he was right up with Moss, who crossed the line just 2/10ths ahead. Stirling had finally won his first World

Championship Grand Prix and had beaten Fangio into the bargain.

That left just the Italian Grand Prix at Monza on 11th September. Moss had a less happy time there. In August, the drivers tested the cars at the Nürburgring and then at Monza, where for the first time, they were using the high speed oval as well as the road circuit (total length 10.042 km.) The oval was bumpy and put a huge strain on tyres and suspension. Mercedes built two streamlined 1954 type cars. The chassis were brought from Stuttgart on a truck powered by a 300 SL engine, which could cruise the autobahns at 160 km/h. Fangio took pole again, ahead of

● **52-53**_Aintree, 16th July 1955: Mercedes totally dominated the British Grand Prix. Here, Fangio leads Moss again. A few laps later the order was reversed and stayed that way to the flag!

● **54**_Aintree, 16th July 1955: a photo signed by the "stars" of the Mercedes team. From left to right, engineer Rudolf Uhlenhaut, Juan Manuel Fangio, Piero Taruffi, Stirling Moss, Karl Kling and Alfred Neubauer. Kling was 3rd and Taruffi 4th. Mercedes-Benz recorded a clean sweep of the top four in the British Grand Prix!

● **55**_Monza, 11th September 1955: for the first time, the Italian Grand Prix was run over a 10.042 km track, including the high speed oval and the road circuit; the point where they joined is shown here, with the streamlined Mercedes of Fangio and Moss leading Taruffi.

Moss and Kling. Moss led from the start. Fangio passed him on the banking and the Mercedes occupied the top four places with Kling and Taruffi in non-streamlined cars. But on lap 19, a stone thrown up by one of Fangio's tyres, broke the wind deflector on Moss' Mercedes. He pitted so the mechanics could change it. Stirling got going again and made up the delay until a piston let go on lap 27. Kling stopped on lap 33 with a transmission failure, while Taruffi finished second, much to the delight of the Italian crowd, ahead of Castellotti's Ferrari. Fangio was World Champion for the third time with 40 points. Moss was runner up on 23 and the Formula 1 season was over.

But there was still endurance racing to deal with. After Le Mans, Moss only raced twice in sports cars, in non-championship events in a Porsche Spyder. His first encounter with this marque came on 24th July when he won in Portugal and then in August, he retired at Goodwood. As for the Mercedes 300 SLRs, they ran on 8th August at Rabelov in Sweden, where Fangio won from Moss. "*It is the only time I can remember getting team orders from Neubauer, to let Fangio win,*" added Moss. Despite pulling out at Le Mans, Mercedes was still in with a chance of the constructors' title, if it took part in the final two rounds: the Tourist Trophy at Dundrod on 17ᵗʰ September and the Targa Florio in Sicily on

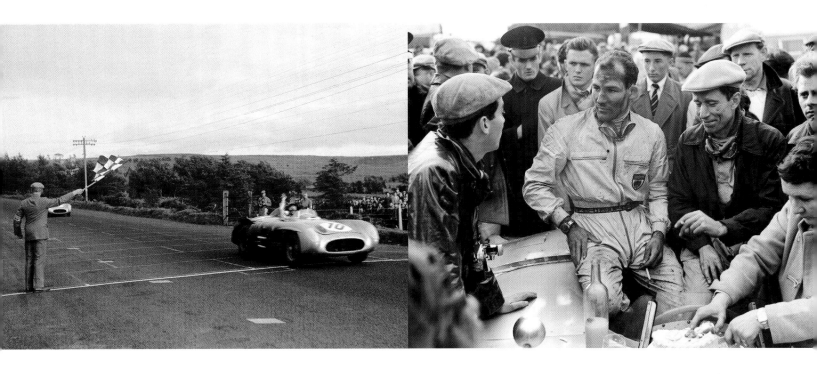

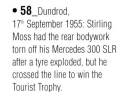

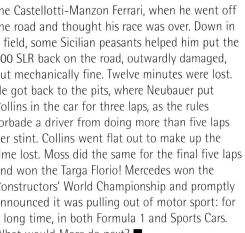

16th October. At Dundrod, a favourite with Moss, his co-driver was the American John Fitch. Moss was leading when a rear tyre exploded. The wing was torn off, but he managed to get back to the pits, where the wheel was changed. Fitch took over, but was now in third place. Neubauer put Moss back out again and he passed Fangio's Mercedes and Hawthorn's Jaguar to win his third Tourist Trophy on his 26th birthday!

Finally, to Sicily, where he chose Peter Collins as his co-driver. The Madonies circuit was 72 kilometres in length, with 800 corners on narrow, bumpy roads. Would it suit the 300 SLR? In the race, Moss made another demon start. On lap 4, he was leading by a healthy margin over the Castellotti-Manzon Ferrari, when he went off the road and thought his race was over. Down in a field, some Sicilian peasants helped him put the 300 SLR back on the road, outwardly damaged, but mechanically fine. Twelve minutes were lost. He got back to the pits, where Neubauer put Collins in the car for three laps, as the rules forbade a driver from doing more than five laps per stint. Collins went flat out to make up the time lost. Moss did the same for the final five laps and won the Targa Florio! Mercedes won the Constructors' World Championship and promptly announced it was pulling out of motor sport: for a long time, in both Formula 1 and Sports Cars. What would Moss do next? ■

● **58**_Dundrod, 17th September 1955: Stirling Moss had the rear bodywork torn off his Mercedes 300 SLR after a tyre exploded, but he crossed the line to win the Tourist Trophy.

● **59**_Dundrod, 17th September 1955: what better way to celebrate his 26th birthday with a win, his third in the Tourist Trophy? Especially as "mummy" Moss cut the birthday cake and served drinks on the bonnet of the 300 SLR! That's what a smiling John Fitch seems to be thinking under his cap. The American was Stirling's co-driver that day. Note the winners all smoking. Different times, different habits. *(The Autocar Editorial)*

● **60**_After the finish of the 39th Targa Florio in the cockpit of the 300 SLR. Moss, still bandaged to protect him from stones, shares the joy of a hard won victory with co-driver Peter Collins. The two men got on famously. *(The Autocar Editorial)*

61_Monaco, 13ᵗʰ May 1956: the style is efficient and unhurried as Moss tackles the Gasometer corner in the splendid works Maserati 250 F. Moss took his second world championship win and even Fangio had to give best.

Chapter 8

1956
With Maserati and against Fangio

At Silverstone, on 22ⁿᵈ November 1955, Moss
tried the three British Formula 1 cars on
offer: the BRM P25, the Connaught and the
Vanwall. All three had four cylinder engines. He
did a 1'50"3 in the Connaught, 1'50"5 in the BRM
and 1'46"9 in the Vanwall. He found good points
with all of them, but none really impressed him.
At least as far as the world championship was
concerned, he doubted their reliability and
wondered what life would be like as part of these
English teams. *"One of the factors was to avoid
being in the same team as Mike Hawthorn or
Peter Collins, who were both mates,"* he admits
today. *"It was better to race against them than
with them."* So, the undecided driver consulted
various specialist journalists. Ferrari? Absolutely
not, having been rebuffed in 1951. Furthermore,
Ferrari had just recruited Fangio. They advised him
to head for Maserati, who had made him an offer
before the Silverstone test. After all, he was on
good terms with the brothers Orsi, the engineer
Giulio Alfieri, the chief tuner Bertocchi and the
sporting director Nello Ugolini who, after a
season with Ferrari, would return to Maserati in
1956. *"Signing for Maserati was like meeting up*

with old friends," said Moss. *"They were adorable,
even if their idea of a contract was not strictly
the same as mine. I had a contract which entitled
me to 50% of the start money. Let's say that a
race was offering a thousand dollars start money,
they would give me four hundred. I'd ask why
and they would say: it's because we had two
hundred dollars worth of expenses. It was the
sort of thing an Englishman would never do. The
mechanics would get very emotional. When the
brake pedal on the 450 S broke on the Mille
Miglia, they were crying!"*

One point of the contract on which both
parties were in full agreement, was the driver's
freedom to drive for other teams and in other
makes of car when Maserati did not enter a team.
This would see Moss drive a Vanwall at
Silverstone in Formula 1. As for Formula Sport,
Moss silenced chauvinistic critics when, after a
February test at Goodwood, he drove some events
for Aston Martin, although he also occasionally
got behind the wheel of Maseratis and Porsches.
This enabled him to gain valuable experience and
to get to grips with other cars, while swelling his
coffers.

The season kicked off with a trip to New Zealand where, on 7th January he raced at the Ardmore aerodrome near Auckland. Stirling scored two wins from two starts, in Formula 1 with his old Maserati 250F and a factory Porsche 1500. Then it was time to fly to Buenos Aires, where he met up with the Maserati team and his team-mates, Jean Behra and Cesare Perdisa. Moss was leading the Argentine Grand Prix on 22nd January, when the engine on his works Maserati 250 F threw a piston, leaving Fangio to win in a Lancia-Ferrari. In the 1000 kilometres race a week later, Moss and Carlos Menditeguy took a 300 S to victory. The 300 S was a superb open seater, with the 6 cylinder engine from the 250 F, bored out to 3 litres. Stirling loved this car, as much as he loved the 250 F with which, on 5th February, he finished second behind Fangio in the Buenos Aires Grand Prix, which strangely enough was run at Mendoza. Moss got his hands on a more powerful version, fitted with injection (chassis 2522) with which he won the Glover Trophy at Goodwood on Easter Monday, after a tooth and nail tussle with Archie Scott-Brown in the Connaught. This amazing gentleman racer was born with a condition which meant he drove with just one arm and had to have the pedals specially modified to cope with his short leg length. These handicaps meant he never raced in the World

Championship Grands Prix, but in England he was a doughty rival to the likes of Moss, Collins, Brooks, Hawthorn and Salvadori.

Honouring his contract, Moss made his Aston Martin debut with the DB3S on 24th March in the Sebring 12 Hours, where he was reunited with his old friend Peter Collins. But the engine broke and so it was at Goodwood that same Easter Monday, that Moss scored his first Aston Martin win, which was also the 100th win of his career, as well as taking pole position and the fastest race lap: "the works" as Moss put it. As a freelance, he finished 4th on 14th April at Oulton Park in the British Empire Trophy with a 1500 cc works Sport Cooper Climax. He ordered one for himself and took it to Aintree on 23rd April. At the same meeting, again in Formula 1, he won the 200 miles race with his old 250 F "2508." It was a hectic and rewarding month of April, apart from the Mille Miglia that is. On 29th April at 5h54, Moss having reformed his legendary partnership with Denis Jenkinson, left Brescia in a works Maserati 350 S (3.5 litres, 6 cylinders, 325 horsepower.) The car was not at all sorted out and they knew it. It would wander all over the road and the front end lifted at anything above 210 km/h, when its 325 horsepower was capable of pushing it along at 260 km/h. Nevertheless, Moss managed to overtake Musso (Ferrari) and

• **63**_Silverstone, 5th May 1956. Moss' first race in a Vanwall "just to see," turned into a first win! The International Trophy did not count towards the World Championship and it was shorter than a grand prix, but the signs were there for the following year.

1956 Italian Grand Prix
Maserati 250F

P.ŕENARD

Designer: Giulio Alfieri

Engine
Make/type: Maserati 250 F
Number of cylinders/configuration: 6 in line (front)
Capacity: 2493.9 cc
Bore x stroke: 84 x 75 mm
Compression ratio: 12:1
Maximum power: 270 horsepower
Maximum revs: 7600 rpm
Block material: light alloy
Carburettors: 3 Weber twin-bodied
Valve gear : twin overhead camshafts
Number of valves per cylinder: 2
Ignition: 2 magnetos (Marelli)
Number of spark plugs per cylinder: 2

Transmission
Gearbox/number of gears: Transverse Maserati (5)
Clutch: Maserati

Chassis
Type: tubular
Suspensions: independent double wishbone front, de Dion rear axle
Dampers: hydraulic (front), leaf spring (rear)
Wheels: 550 x 16 (front) / 700 x 16 (rear)
Tyres: Pirelli
Brakes: Wheel mounted drum brakes (Maserati)

Dimensions
Wheelbase: 2225 mm
Width: 1300 mm (front) / 1250 mm (rear)
Dry weight: 630 kg
Fuel capacity: 200 litres

Used from Argentina to Italy.

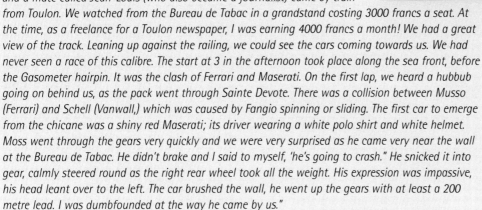
(Photo Christian Bedel)

Johnny Rives
"I was left dumbfounded"

A journalist at "L'Equipe," the French sports daily, Johnny Rives has covered hundreds of grands prix, rallies and endurance races in a long and respected career. From Fangio to Schumacher, Moss to Senna and from Clark to Villeneuve, he has watched all the greats over the past 50 years. His eye-witness account is that of a fan and a professional insider:

"Monaco '56? The scenes that day have stayed in my mind like a film. Me and a mate called Jean-Louis (who also became a journalist) came by train from Toulon. We watched from the Bureau de Tabac in a grandstand costing 3000 francs a seat. At the time, as a freelance for a Toulon newspaper, I was earning 4000 francs a month! We had a great view of the track. Leaning up against the railing, we could see the cars coming towards us. We had never seen a race of this calibre. The start at 3 in the afternoon took place along the sea front, before the Gasometer hairpin. It was the clash of Ferrari and Maserati. On the first lap, we heard a hubbub going on behind us, as the pack went through Sainte Devote. There was a collision between Musso (Ferrari) and Schell (Vanwall,) which was caused by Fangio spinning or sliding. The first car to emerge from the chicane was a shiny red Maserati; its driver wearing a white polo shirt and white helmet. Moss went through the gears very quickly and we were very surprised as he came very near the wall at the Bureau de Tabac. He didn't brake and I said to myself, 'he's going to crash." He snicked it into gear, calmly steered round as the right rear wheel took all the weight. His expression was impassive, his head leant over to the left. The car brushed the wall, he went up the gears with at least a 200 metre lead. I was dumbfounded at the way he came by us."

Perdisa (Maserati 300 S.) They were lying 6th at Pescara, when torrential rain started to fall. The conditions were terrible with nil visibility and very little grip as water began to seep into the cockpit. "Jenks" tried to de-mist his driver's goggles, having handed him a new pair. Then, as they came to a corner, the car skidded and went over a parapet. It came to rest against the only tree around and but for that, the car would have ended up at the bottom of the ravine, 90 metres below.

It is time to talk of less frenetic races, Formula 1 for example. On 5th May, under the agreement with Maserati, who had not entered a team, Moss raced a Vanwall in the International Trophy at Silverstone and won. It was a real boost and he arrived in Monaco a few days later in a strong frame of mind. He was reunited with the Maserati 250 F "2522" which for this event, the factory had fitted with a close ratio 4 speed box. On 13th May, he won the race as described to us by an eye-witness, Johnny Rives (see box above.)

Displaying all the qualities of a world champion in the making, that day saw Moss take the second grand prix win of his career. Fangio, his teacher at Mercedes, went off the track in his Lancia-Ferrari. He took over Peter Collins' car,

with which he staged a remarkable climb through the field, but it was too late to catch Moss, who won by 6 seconds, controlling the race beautifully. Behra came third to add to Maserati's triumph.

Stirling next won the London Trophy at Crystal Palace with his privately entered 250 F. The vagaries of motor racing then found him racing for Maserati on the 27th, in the Nürburgring 1000 kilometres. The works Aston Martin team was also there. Fighting for overall honours were two Maserati 300 S (Moss-Behra and Schell-Taruffi,) up against four 3.5 litre Ferraris, including one for Fangio-Castellotti, who had won the Sebring 12 Hours, two Aston Martin DB3S and two Jaguar D types. Moss drove the first stint and was leading from Fangio's Ferrari when he handed over to Behra on lap 17 of 44. Behra only managed a single lap before a rear spring broke. The Nürburgring track, all 22.810 km of it, was bumpy and boasted 172 corners, which put enormous stress on a car, particularly the chassis. Moss and Behra then helped out, driving the surviving Schell and Taruffi Maserati. Moss drove the final stint, catching up to Fangio, who was forced to refuel, losing the lead to Moss who won by 26 seconds.

• **64**_Monaco, 13th May 1956. Stirling Moss and the Maserati 250 F would seem to be the strongest opposition for Fangio, the Englishman having studied under the master at Mercedes.

● **65**_Spa-Francorchamps, 3rd June 1956: A wet start to the Belgian Grand Prix. Moss' Maserati 250 F (no. 30) lines up between the two Lancia-Ferraris of Fangio (no. 2) and Collins (No. 8.) On the second row, the Lancia-Ferrari of Castellotti (no. 4) and the nose of Behra's Maserati (no. 32.)

After the Nürburgring, it was off to Spa-Francorchamps on 3rd June for the Belgian Grand Prix. In the space of one week, the best drivers in the world were going head to head in two different categories on two of the most beautiful and most dangerous road circuits, located a mere hundred kilometres apart. For the high speed circuit at Spa, Maserati had modified the 250 F with a more profiled nose section, similar to the Vanwalls and air intakes in the bonnet. The experimental "2501" entrusted to Moss also had a redesigned cockpit with a more enclosed windscreen. In qualifying, Moss was second quickest behind Fangio's Lancia-Ferrari and ahead of Hawthorn's BRM and Collins' Lancia-Ferrari. For the race, Moss' Maserati was refitted with Weber

carburettors, as it used too much fuel with the injection system and the Grand Prix was run over a distance of 506.880 km. Moss made an excellent start ahead of Fangio, who then passed again on the drop to Masta. Moss lost a wheel at Eau Rouge, managing to bring the 250 F to a halt with its three remaining wheels. He sprinted the eight hundred metres to the Maserati pits and took over "2522" from Perdisa. Fangio retired with transmission failure and the win went to Peter Collins in the Lancia-Ferrari ahead of the similar car of Paul Frere, the Belgian driver-journalist who had been invited as a guest driver. Moss fought back in his usual manner, beating the lap record on his way to third, sharing 4 points with Perdisa.

There came an interlude in Sports cars, for the "Supercortemaggiore" Grand Prix run on 24th June as a 1000 kilometres race at Monza. Moss was teamed up with Cesare Perdisa in a works 2 litre Maserati 200 S. They finished second. Then it was back to Formula 1 for the ACF Grand Prix at Reims on 1st July. Once again it was a battle between the Maseratis and the Lancia-Ferraris, with the Vanwalls joining in. The French public only had eyes for Maurice Trintignant in the Bugatti 251, which would not get far. Collins took his second win in the World Championship, this time from Castellotti. Fangio ran into problems and drove like a man possessed to finish fourth, close on Behra's heels. And what of Moss? In the leading pack in the early stages, with the Lancia-Ferraris of Gendebien and de Portago, his gear lever broke on lap 12. Once again, it was a sprint on foot to the pits to take over Perdisa's car, with

which he finished fifth, with just two points to split between them. It was a poor weekend as he retired from the 12 Hours of Reims, where he was sharing a Cooper-Climax with the American Phil Hill, when the engine overheated. Consolation came on 8th July at the Rouen-les-Essarts circuit, where Moss finished second behind Castellotti's Ferrari in the Coupe Delamarre-Debouteville in an Aston Martin DB3S. It would serve as a dress rehearsal for the Le Mans 24 Hours.

On 14th July, the British Grand Prix at Silverstone threw up a few oddities: Mike Hawthorn who raced at Reims in a Vanwall, was back at BRM alongside Tony Brooks, known as "the flying dentist" and Ron Flockhart. Vanwall lent a car to the Argentine Froilan Gonzalez who was making a comeback, alongside Maurice Trintignant and Harry Schell. Gordini was trying out the new streamlined single seaters with

● **66**_In the Belgian Grand Prix, Moss lost a wheel at Eau Rouge. He took over the Maserati driven by his young Italian team-mate, Cesare Perdisa. Here, he tackles the La Source hairpin on his way to third after a sprint back through the field.
(Copyright Autosport)

8 cylinder engines, driven by Robert Manzon and Nano da Silva Ramos. At Connaught, Archie Scott-Brown was at the wheel, having been allowed an entry for his home race. Finally, among the fleet of Maserati 250 Fs entered, was one for an almost unknown Australian who worked as a Cooper mechanic: Jack Brabham. But yet again, the key to the race was the eternal battle between the works Ferraris and Maseratis. Moss took pole in 1'41 in a car fitted with carburettors, Maserati having abandoned injection for the time being. Next up was Fangio in 1'42. But at the start, it was the BRMs of Hawthorn and Brooks which shot off into the lead, much to the delight of the home crowd. The delight would be short lived as both cars were eliminated in a spectacular accident. Moss took the lead on lap 16, ahead of Fangio, but he had stop to sort an ignition problem. He set off again, the bit between his teeth and was second when, with

eight laps remaining, his Colotti gearbox broke. *"Typical of a 250 F at the end of a race,"* a downhearted Moss would note, taking consolation from the single point for setting the fastest race lap.

The morning had gone better with victory in the Formula Sport event run as a curtain raiser to the Grand Prix. He also took pole and the fastest race lap. On 22ⁿᵈ July, still in a Maserati 300 S, Stirling repeated that performance in the Bari Grand Prix (Formula Sport.)

The Maserati factory did not take part in the Le Mans 24 Hours, which that year, was held at the end of July, as the circuit, the pits and the grandstands had been extensively modified over a long period of time after the 1955 disaster. In the pouring rain, the race was won by an Ecurie Ecosse Jaguar D type after two works Jaguars and a Ferrari had retired in the early stages in an accident; luckily there were no injuries. Moss and

his friend Peter Collins were driving a factory Aston Martin DB3S. The team was run by John Wyer, an experienced, authoritative team boss with plenty of experience, who was also an affable bon viveur. *"He knew all the good hotels and restaurants and looked after his drivers wellbeing,"* said an appreciative Stirling, who rated him as highly as Alfred Neubauer. The car was an open seater fitted with an in-line 3 litre, 6 cylinder engine, putting out around 240 horsepower. It was slower than the Jaguar D type, but thanks to the rain, Moss and Collins were able to mix it with the Ecurie Ecosse Jaguar D type, driven by Ron Flockhart and Ninian Sanderson. They were even leading at the halfway mark. Shortly after that, Collins screamed into the pits indicating that he could no longer select second gear. It cost them one and a half laps and the win. They finished second behind the Jaguar. On 18th August, at Oulton Park, Moss won the Daily

Herald Trophy in a DB3S. Stirling came back from Le Mans having fallen in love. When Collins was at the wheel, on Saturday before nightfall, watching from the Aston Martin pits, Stirling noted a very pretty young woman with short hair watching the race from the grandstand. They communicated in sign language and, as she did not have a pass, Stirling went over to meet her and they swapped addresses. She was called Kate Molson, the heir to a famous Canadian brewery company. She was soon to become Stirling's first wife.

The next Formula 1 appointment was the German Grand Prix, on 5th August at the Nürburgring. Here too, Moss raced in the up to 1500 cc Sport race as a curtain raiser in a Maserati 150 S. He finished second, just as he would in the grand prix. In qualifying, Fangio took pole. Fourth placed Moss was the only "non-Ferrari." In the race, he was powerless against

● **68**_Silverstone, 14th July 1956: Later in the day, he would retire on lap 68 of the British Grand Prix with a broken gearbox. For the moment, Stirling savours victory in the Formula Sport race, the curtain raiser to the main event, in a Maserati 300 S.

● **69**_Le Mans, 28th July
1956: the Le Mans 24 Hours
was run later than usual this
year because of improvements
to the circuit. Stirling shared
this Aston Martin DB3S with
Peter Collins and matched his
1953 performance, finishing
second behind a Jaguar.
(Quadrant Picture Library)

Fangio. But Moss hung on for dear life and
finished 47" down. Behra in another Maserati was
next, seven minutes behind the leader! Only five
finishers were classified.

That left the Italian Grand Prix at Monza on
2nd September. On this occasion Maserati had
decided to put on a show. There were two new
250 F cars for Moss (chassis 2525) and Behra
(2526.) The chassis had been widened and
lowered. The engine had been moved sideways
and the drive shaft passed alongside the driver,
which meant the seat could be lowered, lowering
the centre of gravity by 20 centimetres. The race
order changed several times and the result would
decide the outcome of the world championship.
Moss started from the second row behind the

Lancia-Ferraris of Fangio, Musso and Castellotti.
The two Italians shot off like rockets and ruined
their tyres. Moss then found himself in the lead,
chased by Harry Schell in the Vanwall and Fangio.
The Argentine was later forced to stop and, as is
well known, took over Peter Collins' car. As Moss
led the Italian Grand Prix from Schell, he beat the
lap record on lap 47. Then, the Maserati's engine
began to splutter. It had run out of fuel with just
three laps to go! Luigi Piotti then arrived on the
scene in a privately entered 250 F. Moss indicated
what had happened and the Italian carefully
nudged the nose of his car into the back of
Stirling's and pushed the Englishman to the pit
lane entry. A few litres of fuel were hastily poured
in and Moss charged off to win the grand prix

with a 5.7 second lead over Fangio, who took the World Championship for the fourth time, with 33 points, ahead of Moss on 28. The tifosi were delighted. Stirling Moss was a very busy man and, for him, the season never ended with the Formula 1 World Championship. The day after the Italian Grand Prix, he was still at Monza to set some Class G records (50 km at 135.54 mph and the 50 miles at 132.77 mph) with a Lotus-Climax type 11 with an 1100 cc engine. A fortnight later, he filled a week competing in the Tour de France at the wheel of a Mercedes 300 SL coupe supplied by Georges Houel, a pretty decent rally driver and motor cyclist, who later went into the restaurant business. "Le Volant," in the 15th arrondissement of Paris became a popular watering hole with any racing drivers passing through. *"I was struck by Moss' organisational ability and attention to detail,"* recalled Houel.

"He left nothing to chance. For example, we were sharing a hotel room and at the end of every leg, he would completely unpack his suitcase, repacking it in the same order the following morning." The Tour de France started from Nice and included a series of timed sections, linked by road sections, with some hillclimbs and race circuits thrown in. Moss drove the Mercedes brilliantly to give Alfonso de Portago/Ed Nelson a hard time in the Ferrari 250 GT. In the end, victory went to the Ferrari after the 300 SL had lost ground due to a badly adjusted ignition. Moss was back in a Maserati 300 S to win the Formula Sport Grand Prix in Caracas, Venezuela on 4th November and in Melbourne, Australia on the 25th. Still in Melbourne, he won the Formula 1 Australian Grand Prix in a 250 F on 2nd December. But his thoughts were already turning to another F1 car: a green one. ■

• **70**_Monza, 2nd September 1956: a close win for Moss and his Maserati 250 F, after getting a push from Piotti in a private Maserati. Stirling fought like a lion for the win. It was the day Fangio finished second in the Italian and European Grand Prix, having taken over Collins' Lancia-Ferrari to become World Champion for the fourth time.

Chapter 9
1957-1958
Mr. Vandervell's bearings

● **71**_Pescara, 18th August 1957: in this "Italian Grand Prix Mk 2," held on a 25 kilometres circuit, part town and part countryside, Moss and his Vanwall gave the opposition no chance, not even the Maserati of Fangio, the recently crowned five times World Champion!

• **72**_Sebring, 23rd March
1957: in the 12 Hours, Moss is
seen at the wheel of the superb
Maserati 300 S which he
shared with Harry Schell. They
finished second behind the
Fangio-Behra 450 S.
(Bernard Cahier Archives)

Guy Anthony Vandervell, who answered to "Tony" was born in 1898. He was the son of an industrialist with links to the automobile industry which dated back to before the war. He was the head of a company which specialised in producing thinwall bearings. In 1948, he was one of the first to back the BRM project, joining its board of directors. But he pulled out the following year, citing the company's lack of direction and no doubt wishing to avoid getting embroiled in a power struggle with Raymond Mays and Peter Berthon. He then set up his own race team, running 12 cylinder Ferraris, as he provided the Italian firm with bearings. He produced an evolution of the 4.5 litre 375 F1 known as the "Thin Wall Special," which he entered in Formula Libre races. Then in 1953, he built a Formula 2 engine, based on the Manx Norton 500 cc single. According to Christian Moity, writing in the *"Automobile Historique"* magazine, *"he was ambitious, but more in terms of his country than for any personal reputation, as he was already a part of the establishment. He was authoritarian, impulsive and sometimes even irascible."* In racing terms, his major preoccupation was with those who took the risks, namely the drivers.

The Vanwalls had their suspension and aerodynamics tweaked by Colin Chapman, the Lotus boss, who had a special contract with them and his aerodynamicist friend Frank Costin. The car had a fantastic bullet-shaped profile which saw it touch speeds of 290 km/h on the quick tracks. At Spa, Reims and Monza, Schell's Vanwall left Moss' Maserati for dead. The Vanwalls were fragile and experienced highs and lows in the 1956 Grands Prix. Their best result was a 4th place for Harry Schell in Belgium. But ever since Moss won the International Trophy at Silverstone, in May 1956, he was convinced of the car's potential. On 10th October 1956, Stirling had a quick test in a Vanwall at Silverstone, Then, on 22nd October, he ran one over a grand prix distance at Oulton Park. He signed a contract with Tony Vandervell's team, then run by David Yorke. With Hawthorn back at Ferrari and Schell at Maserati, the other drivers would be Tony Brooks and Stuart Lewis-Evans, who would move later from Connaught. Moss was contracted to drive in World Championship events for Vanwall, unless the team was not entered. That was the case in Argentina on 13th January 1957. So, with Vandervell's approval, he raced the Maserati again, setting the fastest race lap before retiring. Then he won the Formula Sport Buenos Aires 1000 kilometres, the Cuban Grand Prix in Havana and the Sebring 12 Hours, all with Maserati.

He was back with the Vanwall team in Europe for the Syracuse Grand Prix in Sicily on 7th April. It was a handy way of getting his eye in before Monaco. Starting from the front row, an on-form Moss was leading Collins in the Ferrari when on lap 32, a broken oil line meant he had to make a pit stop. The problem was fixed very quickly and Stirling was back in the race in seventh place. He beat the lap record and climbed as high as third. It was obvious that with a bit of development, the Vanwall was capable of beating the Ferraris and Maseratis; *"those bloody red cars,"* as Mr. Vandervell was fond of repeating. The next challenge would come in Monaco on 19th May. Before then, there was the Mille Miglia to contend with.

These days, a Formula 1 driver can hardly go to the toilet or reveal to the media what his favourite food is without it being written into his contract. Hard to imagine therefore that, forty years ago, a driver could compete in the F1 World Championship for one make of car and then take part in a Sports Car series at the wheel of a rival marque. But that is exactly what Moss did when, after driving in Buenos Aires and Sebring, he was back at the wheel of a Maserati 450 S in Brescia for the start of the Millie Miglia, teamed up once again with his friend Denis Jenkinson. The car was a fearsome beast, a powerful monster; its 4.5 litre V8 putting out over 400 horsepower which could propel it to speeds of 290 km/h. It was the very same specification as the one used by Fangio and Behra to win in Sebring. Moss did not like this car, finding it too heavy. He much preferred the agile and efficient 300 S. But a contract is a contract

and past experience had shown that Moss had no qualms about taming recalcitrant beasts on open roads, as he had done with the 350 S in 1956. The car was well prepared and he started as favourite, but it was all over after just seven kilometres. The brake pedal had been drilled for lightness and it snapped off at the base, when the driver was travelling at 230 km/h. Moss and "Jenks" crawled dejectedly back to Brescia, where on finding out what had happened, the mechanics all burst into tears! A few hours later, the news broke that the Portago-Nelson Ferrari had gone off into the crowd, shortly before the finish. Eleven spectators were dead. It was the end of the Mille Miglia. At Monaco, Fangio took pole ahead of Collins and Moss, making it one Maserati, one Ferrari and one Vanwall on the front row. It was a fine sight. Moss led from the start ahead of Fangio and Collins. On lap 4, going into the harbour chicane, the Vanwall's brakes failed and with rear braking only the car went into a slide. Fangio, as calm and quick thinking as ever, managed to avoid it on his way to winning, but Collins hit it from behind and an unsighted Hawthorn could not avoid the carnage. The incident left three top drivers, two Ferraris and a Vanwall out of the running. Tony Brooks saved the day for Vanwall and for the English drivers, coming home behind an imperious Fangio, repeating his 1950 performance.

● **73**_Monaco, 19th May 1957: a Grand Prix to forget for Moss. The Vanwall, with a modified bonnet featuring a large air intake, went off the road with brake failure, taking the Ferraris of Hawthorn and Collins with it. Stirling was slightly injured on the nose.

Another endurance race and again in the Maserati 450 S. Moss was teamed up with Fangio for the Nürburgring 1000 Km. On lap 8, he was leading when he lost a wheel at Schwalbenschwanz! He limped back to the pits and got behind the wheel of Schell's 450 S. That broke too. Two 450 S were entered for the Le Mans 24 Hours: an open version and an aerodynamic coupe designed by Frank Costin and built by Zagato. Fangio tried it in practice, but reckoned it was dangerous. He put himself down as reserve driver in the open car of Behra and Simon. Moss was put in the coupe with Schell. At the end of the first hour he was running third, struggling with the effects of toxic fumes leaking into the cockpit! He then handed over to Schell, but the engine broke soon after.

The summer had got off to a bad start, as during a short holiday on the Cote d'Azur, with his fiancee Katie Molson, he tried to pull off a trick on water skis and got water up his nose. The doctor diagnosed severe sinusitis, which put him out of the ACF Grand Prix, held at Rouen-les-Essarts and won by Fangio. Stirling also missed a

non-championship Grand Prix at Reims, Stirling was determined to make his mark, when he returned for the British Grand Prix to be run at Aintree. He was particularly keen to do well as poor Tony Brooks was recovering from an accident at Le Mans in an Aston Martin and was unlikely to go the distance. Later we will hear what Tony Brooks had to say about it, but let us just note that the weekend which looked like going badly for the two Vanwall friends would end in triumph.

To start with in Thursday practice, they were left for dead by Fangio and Behra in the Maseratis. The next day, Moss took pole in 2'00"2. Starting alongside him were Behra and Brooks. The young Stuart Lewis-Evans, who had replaced Moss at Rouen and Reims had done enough to earn his spurs with the team. He was not far off, a second down on Moss, who took the lead as the flag dropped. On lap 20, he had a 9 second lead over Behra when the Vanwall's engine began to misfire. A pit stop to cure the problem dropped Moss to 7th place. A few laps later, Moss cruised round to the pits again. Brooks pitted and handed

• **74**_Le Mans, 22nd July 1957: for the 24 Hours, Stirling was teamed up with Harry Schell to drive the monstrous Maserati 450 S with a coupe body finished in haste, or rather not finished at all, by Zagato. He retired after a heroic start to the race with exhaust fumes filling the cockpit!

• **75**_Aintree, 20th July 1957: Tony Brooks, suffering from injuries sustained in an accident at Le Mans, was powerless to fight off Mike Hawthorn's Ferrari (no. 10) in the British Grand Prix.

• **76-77**_Brooks has just stopped. The Vanwall is refuelled and Moss jumps into the cockpit. The British Grand Prix is on again!

• **78**_Thanks to a meteoric climb through the field, using every inch of the track, Stirling took Vanwall no. 20 to victory with a 25"6 lead over Musso's Ferrari.

• **79-80**_History is made! For the first time since Henry Segrave in a Sunbeam at San Sebastian in 1924, a British driver (two of them actually, Brooks handing over to Moss) wins a "Grande Epreuve." The icing on the cake: it's the home Grand Prix.
(79: The Autocar Editorial)

his "VW4" to Moss, trying to continue in "VW1" with the faulty magneto. It did not want to know. But "VW4" was fine and just getting into its stride after a stop lasting just 13 seconds. Seventh on lap 30, one minute down on Behra, Moss was on the limit. He beat the lap record and Behra responded. Moss lowered the record to 1'59"2 – quicker than in qualifying. With 22 laps remaining he had closed to within 28 seconds of Behra. The pace was stunning and the excitement reached its peak when Behra retired with a cooked clutch on the Maserati. Could Moss catch Hawthorn's Ferrari, who was now the leader? Hawthorn had to stop and change a wheel after a puncture and the Vanwall was leading! Lewis-Evans had to stop to adjust his throttle and Moss was now out of Hawthorn's clutches, who had rejoined third and simply had to fend off Musso, who finished 26 seconds behind him. It was the first 100% British win –both car and driver – since Henry Segrave took a Sunbeam to victory in the Spanish Grand Prix at San Sebastian in 1924. But this time, it was even more of a milestone as it was the British Grand Prix! Moss described this day as *"one of the most satisfying of my entire career."*

On 4th August, at the German Grand Prix, Moss, Brooks and Lewis-Evans realised that the Vanwall suspension was too hard to deal with the bumps and cambers of the Nürburgring. While Fangio scored his most famous win, Lewis-Evans went off the road, Brooks finished 9th and Moss wore himself out to come home 5th, just one second ahead of Behra, whom he passed in the final long straight before the finish.

But the Italians had seen nothing yet and they would see everything at home. In the space of a fortnight, Moss and Vanwall would strike two significant blows. At Pescara on 18th August, on a 25 kilometres track, a grand prix was organised after the Belgian and Dutch Grands Prix were cancelled. Moss started from the front row between Fangio and Musso (in the only Ferrari.) Moss won having passed Musso on lap 2, beating the Maseratis of Fangio and Schell after Behra retired. He also set a lap record. Fangio was 3 minutes down! At Monza, on 18th September, the three Vanwalls were fastest in qualifying. Lewis-Evans was on pole position, ahead of Moss and Brooks. Fangio was fourth in the Maserati; the only dash of red on the front row, which it is

• **81**_Tony Brooks (on left,) Stirling Moss and, waving the winner's trophy, Tony Vandervell: two drivers and a happy constructor.

Tony Brooks
Two Vanwalls on the front row

The man whom Stirling Moss referred to as *"the best underrated driver"* gave us this eye witness account of the 1957 British Grand Prix:

"The race took place on 20th July, less than four weeks after Le Mans, where I had been trapped under an Aston Martin DBR 1, bearing some of its quite considerable weight. I had serious cuts with a big hole punched in my right thigh and when I was just about fit enough to drive, even if it was only a road car, it was time to go to official practice on the Thursday before the race. I was in no fit state to race, even if I was able to convince the doctors otherwise. Vanwall did not have a good reliability record at the time and so the idea was to get three cars to the start to increase the chances of success. With the help of some big rubber adhesive bandages to reduce the pressure on my wounds, I managed to set the second quickest time in qualifying, equally the lap record, two tenths of a second slower than Stirling Moss on pole position, which meant there were two Vanwalls on the front row. Before the race, I made it clear to the team that I was not fit enough to do 90 laps at racing speed, but that I would keep the car well placed so that one of my team-mates (Stuart Lewis-Evans was the third driver) could take it over if one of their cars was giving trouble. I brought the car back for Stirling on lap 26, in fifth place, within catching distance of the leaders.
There had been no question of Stirling taking over my car under normal circumstances, because there were only tenths of a second difference between our lap times in qualifying and more than once it was in my favour.
Stirling made a big contribution to Vanwall's success in '57 and '58 of course and we shared the cake equally in '58 with three wins each in the Grands Prix, which brought the team the Constructors' World Championship."

• **82**_Nürburgring, 4th August 1957: a less happy German Grand Prix because of suspension which could not cope with the pitfalls of this very tough track. Stirling had to settle for 5th place. The winner that day was Fangio, driving in a state of grace.

• **83**_Pescara, 18th August 1957: Moss and his Vanwall were simply unbeatable on the day. Starting from second (Fangio was on pole in the Maserati) he finished the Grand Prix, run in torrid heat on a long track, with a 3'13"9 lead over Fangio.
(The Autocar Editorial)

• **84**_A very beautiful and rare rear three quarter shot of Moss' Vanwall at the Pescara circuit, which was largely unknown as it was rarely used for the World Championship.

• **85**_At the finish, exhaustion is written all over the winner's face.

● **86**_Monza, 2ⁿᵈ September 1957: just before the start of the Italian Grand Prix, from left to right, the Vanwalls of Lewis-Evans (no. 20,) Moss (no.18) and Brooks (no. 22.) On the right, Fangio's Maserati (no. 2) saved Italian honour.

claimed the organisers "widened" specifically to ensure this happened! Moss was worried at the start of the race as a stiff gearbox meant he was struggling to select the gears. Lewis-Evans stopped to adjust his steering and Brooks his throttle. Ah, the lack of reliability of the Vanwalls! Moss managed to maintain a 5 second lead over Fangio and Behra. On the day, the Ferraris were off the pace. As for Maserati, their threat evaporated when Fangio stopped to change tyres, followed by Behra retiring with an over-heating engine. Moss had won the Italian Grand Prix in an English car, a year after victory here in an Italian one. However, it was not enough to make him World Champion. That went to the incredible Fangio, who secured his fifth and final title with 46 points (40 retained,) and Moss on 25, runner up for the third time. At the time, no one knew Fangio would announce his retirement in 1958, but it was blindingly obvious that Moss was his natural successor.

In between his two Italian triumphs, the indefatigable Stirling found the time to fly off to the United States, heading for the Bonneville salt lake in Utah, where he beat several records in an experimental MG, the streamlined EX 181: the kilometre at 245.6 mph up to the 10 kilometres at 224.7 mph. Just after the Italian Grand Prix, he set off for another Tour de France in a Mercedes 300 SL and finished fourth, this time with the

journalist Peter Garnier sitting alongside him. On 7ᵗʰ October in London, Stirling and Katie were married. The witnesses were Peter Collins and Mike Hawthorn. After the ceremony at Saint Peter's church, there was an extravagant reception at the Dorchester. The wedding attracted a society crowd as well as the racing folk and featured heavily in the popular press. The newlyweds flew off for a brief honeymoon in Amsterdam, before heading for Casablanca for the Moroccan Grand Prix on 27ᵗʰ October. It was a non-championship event, but news had broken that it would be the final event of the 1958 series. Hence, Moss and the other drivers were keen to discover the Ain Diab circuit. However, having got there, he had to drop out because of a bad dose of 'flu. But he did meet up with Rob Walker, one of the heirs to the Johnny Walker whisky company and the owner of a Formula 2 team running Cooper-Climax cars, who wanted to move up to Formula 1. The two men agreed on a handshake that Moss would race for Walker in 1958 in Formula 2 on a regular basis and in Formula 1, when Vanwall, his priority team, was not entered.

Next stop, Caracas, with Katie going along. The Sport Grand Prix of Venezuela was held on 3ʳᵈ November, run over 1000 kilometres as the last round of the Constructors' World Championship, to be decided between Ferrari and Maserati. It turned into a personal catastrophe for Moss and for the Maserati team as a whole. Moss, who had got his old mate Brooks roped into the affair, as Aston Martin was not taking part, was leading in a 450 S ahead of the 4 litre Ferraris of Collins and Hawthorn. Then, on lap 33 an amateur American racer, Max Dressel, lost control of his AC Bristol right in front of Moss, who was unable to avoid running into him. Dressel was seriously hurt and Moss was deeply affected when he later heard the news. He got back to the pits and took over a 450 S from Schell who had been slightly burnt when the car caught fire, as was Behra. A bit later, out on the track, the 450 S caught fire again, right behind the driver. Schell then took over from Moss, also burnt, but the 450 S was hit by Joachim Bonnier's 300 S. Three factory Maseratis were destroyed, Ferrari won the race and the championship and it is said that this catastrophe pushed the trident marque towards bankruptcy. True or false, Maserati went into receivership in 1958.

In December, Moss and Katie had a holiday in the sunny Bahamas. He found time to race, without success, in the Nassau Tourist Trophy and finished fourth in the Governor's Trophy in an Aston Martin DBR 2. The car was damaged in the hands of another driver in another race. Moss switched to a Ferrari 290 S (3.5 litre V12,) lent by the privateer Jan de Vroom. A win in a minor event, but his first in a Ferrari. It would not be his last... ■

● **87**_After the finish of the Italian Grand Prix, Moss reaps the spoils of victory from his fiancee Katie Molson. *(Associated Press Photo from London)*

Chapter 10
1958
The one who "should have"

For 1958, the CSI (Commission Sportive Internationale, the equivalent of today's FIA) announced three important modifications to the rules for Grand Prix World Championship: first of all the races would be run over a distance of between 300 and 400 kilometres, as opposed to 500; secondly, Av Gas (aviation fuel) was now the only fuel allowed and thirdly, a Constructors' Cup was established. Vanwall and BRM were not ready for the off and missed the Argentine Grand Prix which was the season opener at Buenos Aires on 19th January. Moss' contract allowed him to compete with another marque and he signed up with Rob Walker to drive a Cooper-Climax; a 1500 cc Formula 2 car originally, fitted with a 1960 cc Climax FPF engine. The Coventry factory had not yet produced that size of engine and the modification was carried out by Alf Francis, who was now Rob Walker's chief mechanic at his workshop in Dorking. Jack Brabham used the car at Brands Hatch for the Boxing Day race, then Alf changed the jets on the Weber carburettors to suit the new fuel. Incredible by today's standards, the car was never tested before being flown to Buenos Aires, where Stirling and Katie joined Alf and his Australian assistant Tim Wall, while Rob Walker stayed in England. In the absence of BRM, its drivers for 1958, Behra and Schell, were still entered by Maserati and there were only ten cars at the start, which cast doubt over the event's credentials as a World Championship Grand Prix. To add insult to injury, Stirling had damaged an eye a few days earlier and his vision was slightly blurred. In the first practice session, he complained about poor handling, especially in the fast corners. The next day, thanks to some fettling from Alf, the handling had improved, but Moss was only seventh in 1"4." His Climax engine only put out 165 horsepower, compared with 270 for the Maseratis and 290 for the V6 Dino Ferrari and he did not hold out any hope of winning. His new Continental tyres had a life expectancy of around 40 laps, but after discussions with Alf, he had decided to go the full 80 laps without changing them, as the Cooper wheels were fixed with four nuts and the change would lose two minutes. The gamble paid off with an unexpected win. On lap 4,

● **88**_Casablanca, 19th October 1958: in the Vanwall at the peak of his powers, Moss won the Moroccan Grand Prix and set the fastest race lap. It would not be enough to prevent Mike Hawthorn becoming World Champion.

● **89**_Buenos Aires,
19ᵗʰ January 1958: another
historic win for Moss in the
Argentine Grand Prix. It was the
first for a Cooper (run by Rob
Walker) and the first for a rear-
engined car in the World
Championship.
(The Autocar Editorial)

Moss' gearbox jammed in second, because of a clutch problem. He did one lap like this and headed for the pits, when the box sorted itself out on its own! A stone had hit the Cooper and by some miracle had freed the clutch. The gearbox was working perfectly again and Moss passed Musso, then Behra. He was third and passed Hawthorn's Ferrari, which was following Fangio, in the lead in the Maserati. Moss went as fast as he could down the straights, but tried to save the tyres through the corners. Fangio stopped to change his tyres on lap 35, handing Moss the lead. On lap 54, it was Musso, on fresh rubber, who attacked the under-powered Cooper. Moss was constantly watching his tyre wear, as white patches began to appear on their contact patches, then lines, then whole strips of canvas thread! He was losing at least one second per lap and he occasionally moved off the racing line to run on the oily part of the track to look after what was left of his tyres. Musso was closing. The gamble was going to pay off, but they had called everyone's bluff as Alf had laid out a set of new wheels in the pit lane, ostensibly ready to make a pit stop, but both he and Moss knew it was not going to happen. The Italian had left his charge too late and finished 2"7 behind the Englishman at the line. It was the first win for a Cooper and,

more importantly, the first for a rear engined car in a Formula 1 Grand Prix. Justice was served as a Monaco meeting of the CSI decided that the Argentine Grand Prix would count for championship points.

A week later, Moss was teamed with Jean Behra in a Porsche 1600 RSK for the 1000 Kilometres of Buenos Aires, the first round of the Sports Cars Constructors' World Championship. They enjoyed a great fight with the 3 litre Ferraris of Collins-Phil Hill and Gendebien-Von Trips and finished third, just 9 seconds behind the second Ferrari. A few days later, at the Grand Prix of Buenos Aires (Formula Libre,) Moss' Cooper was hit from behind by a local driver, out of control in the wet. Moss was shaken up and the car was rebuilt at Rob Walker's using a new chassis. In the meantime, it was time for the Cuban Grand Prix (sports cars) on 23ʳᵈ February in Havana. On the eve of this race, Fangio was kidnapped by Castro's "barbudos." The Argentine champion, who was freed the next day, was able to persuade his captors not to take Moss as well. As the driver revealed, *"Fangio told them: 'you've already got me and Moss is on holiday here with his young wife and she will be worried. You don't need him as well.' You can understand why I have infinite respect for Fangio to this day."*

Moss therefore raced in Havana, in a borrowed Ferrari 335 S. The race was red flagged after a dramatic accident on lap 5, when a car ploughed into the crowd, killing six spectators. Moss was declared the winner, ahead of Masten Gregory. The American reproached the Englishman for having profited from the confusion to overtake him just before the finish line. The two rivals sorted out their differences by playing poker with their winnings. On 23rd March in the Sebring 12 Hours, Aston Martin turned up with the DBR 1 for Moss-Brooks and Salvadori-Shelby. Moss led for a long time and set a lap record, but the Aston's gearbox packed in and the Ferraris won. It was a similar scenario on 11th May at the Targa Florio in Sicily, where Moss was slowed down by a stupid problem when the fan failed. He staged a desperate charge through the field, breaking the lap record on the way, before the Aston gearbox packed up yet again. Ferrari won the race and extended its lead in the world championship.

Finally, at Monaco on 18th May, the F1 World Championship got underway for real, with all competitors reporting for duty. In the non-championship 200 Miles at Aintree on 19th April, Stirling raced Rob Walker's rebuilt Cooper, with a 2015 cc engine this time. He beat Jack Brabham's works Cooper after a thrilling dice. For Monaco, the Aintree Cooper was entrusted to Maurice Trintignant. Indeed, Vanwall was back with three

cars for Moss, Brooks and Lewis-Evans. Pole position went to Brooks in 1'39"8, ahead of Behra (BRM) and Brabham in the new Cooper with a 2.2 litre Climax engine. Moss was eighth on the grid, passed Trintignant and Salvadori and then attacked Behra followed by Hawthorn, whom he passed on lap 32. The Vanwalls of Lewis-Evans and Brooks had retired, but the man in the white helmet was leading the Grand Prix. It was not to last: on lap 38, a valve burnt out on the Vanwall, handing the lead to Hawthorn's Ferrari, but that also retired a few laps later with fuel pump problems. It was ironic therefore that Trintignant, who had played a waiting game, took the lead and kept it to the flag. It was the second Monaco win for the Frenchman, who had triumphed with Ferrari in 1955 and it was also the second consecutive win for Rob Walker's Cooper. John Cooper, who was in the process of revolutionising Formula 1 was peeved, as it was not his cars doing the winning. The other constructors were also worried, asking themselves just how far these strange little machines would go.

As for Moss, he was hungrier than ever for revenge, whether it was in a front or rear engined car. In qualifying for the Dutch Grand Prix at Zandvoort on 26th May, Vanwall hit home yet again. It was shades of Monza '57, with three English cars on the front row of the grid. And just like Monza, it was the young Stuart Lewis-Evans

● **90**_Zandvoort, 26th May 1958: at the start of the Dutch Grand Prix, Moss (Vanwall no. 1) went straight into the lead, ahead of Lewis-Evans (Vanwall no. 3) and the rest of the pack.

● **91**_A stylish Moss at the wheel of the Vanwall in the Dutch Grand Prix, which he won as he pleased. Note the non-spoked rear wheels on this evolution of the car.
(The Autocar Editorial)

who took pole in 1'37"1, ahead of Moss (1'38") and Brooks (1'38"1.) Stirling went into the lead at the start and stayed there. Brooks retired and Lewis-Evans was passed by Schell (BRM) and Salvadori (Cooper.) Of the three Vanwalls, this time it was Moss' which kept going to the end. He beat the lap record on the penultimate lap, having run a perfect race ahead of the BRMs of Schell and Behra and Salvadori's Cooper. The first non-English car was Hawthorn's Ferrari, down in 5th place.

On 1st June, Moss was back in Formula Sport mode for the Nürburgring 1000 Kilometres. This time, he was paired with none other than his

Formula 1 rival, Jack Brabham, making his debut in the Aston Martin DBR 1. Stirling was very keen to do well here after the races in Florida and Sicily had only promised to deceive. Between the two practice sessions, he got the new team boss Reg Parnell to change the final drive on the Aston, as it was only pulling 5900 rpm in fifth, in order to reach the desired 6500 rpm. He led from the start, but when Jack Brabham took over, the Australian could not match his pace and was passed by the Ferraris of Hawthorn and Von Trips. In the space of 3 laps, the Aston lost 30 seconds to the lead Ferrari. After 3 laps, Brabham stopped to change tyres and refuel. An angry Moss got

1958
Vanwall VW 10
Portuguese Grand Prix

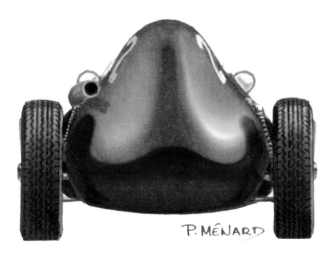

P. MÉNARD

Designers: Colin Chapman and Harry Weslake

Engine
Make/type: Vanwall
Number of cylinders/configuration: 4 in line (front)
Capacity: 2490 cc
Bore x stroke: 96 x 86 mm
Compression ratio: 11:1
Maximum power: 265 horsepower (on Avgas)
Maximum revs: 7400 rpm
Block: alloy
Fuel supply: Bosch direct injection
Valve drive: 2 overhead cams
Number of valves per cylinder: 2
Number of spark plugs per cylinder: 2
Ignition: Bosch double magneto

Transmission
Gearbox/number of gears: Vanwall/5
Clutch: Vanwall multi-plate

Chassis
Type: multi-tubular structure
Suspension: independent front; de Dion rear axle
Dampers: telescopic, helical springs
Tyres: Dunlop 5.50 x 16 (front) / 700 x 16 (rear)
Brakes: discs front and rear

Dimensions
Wheelbase: 2280 mm
Width: 1355 (front) / 1320 (rear)
Dry weight: 550 kg
Fuel capacity: 180 litres

Used from Monaco to Morocco

• **92**_Moss at the wheel of the sole remaining Vanwall in the Dutch Grand Prix. He beat the lap record on his penultimate lap. Note how close the photographer is standing (on right.)

back behind the wheel and began to reel in the Ferraris, passed them and tore off into the distance. He handed over to Brabham, who did another five laps, managing to stay in the lead this time. Moss was back at the wheel for the final eleven laps, beating Hawthorn and the Ferraris, having worn himself out with the effort. *"That day, I drove 36 of the 44 laps in the race and it took me a week to recover,"* he recounted. *"I was more pumped up about this win than the one in the Mille Miglia in 1955."*

The season continued apace, even if it did so with a defeat, just as significant as the two wins. Even the greatest drivers get it wrong. At the Belgian Grand Prix, Stirling would prove that. At Spa-Francorchamps, another circuit where bravery comes to the fore, just as it did at the Nürburgring 1000 Kilometres a week earlier.

Stirling started from the front row alongside pole-man Hawthorn and Musso in the Ferrari. He took the lead, but accelerating out of Stavelot, 200 metres ahead of the Ferraris, he stayed in fourth gear, up to 7200 rpm, but failed to select fifth correctly. When he floored the throttle, he found himself in neutral. The over-revved engine expired on the spot. Forty years later, Moss was still angry with himself: *"I was upset by what I had done. It was entirely my fault."* Fortunately for Vanwall, Brooks won the race, with Lewis-Evans third. But Hawthorn was second, picking up 7 points. Moss had just stupidly compromised his championship chances.

Between the Belgian and ACF Grands Prix, a very special race took place at Monza, run in three legs, over the high-speed oval, run in the opposite direction to usual. "It was the "Race of

• **93**_Nürburgring, 1ˢᵗ June 1958: Stirling Moss' Aston Martin in full flight on the toboggan at the Eifel. Partnered by Jack Brabham, on his debut at this track and in this car, Stirling would give his all to win this classic endurance race.

• **94**_After the finish of the Nürburgring 1000 Km, Moss and Brabham with Reg Parnell; all smiles after beating the factory Ferraris.
(Quadrant Picture Library)

● **95**_Monza, 29th June 1958:
in the "Race of the two Worlds,"
Moss was at the wheel of this
Maserati "Eldorado Special,"
fitted with a 4.2 litre V8, as in
Formula Indy. He shone in the
race before a frightening crash
from which he miraculously
escaped.
(The Autocar Editorial)

the two Worlds," planned to bring together
Formula 1 drivers and their American cousins in
Formula "Indy" cars. It did not count towards any
championship, but the prize money was generous.
Fangio drove an American roadster, while Ferrari
and Maserati prepared special cars for Musso and
Moss respectively. The Maserati was called
"Eldorado" after its main sponsor, an ice cream
manufacturer. It was fitted with the 450 S V8
engine bored out to 4.2 litres for the occasion.
Fourth in the first leg, fifth in the second, Moss
got the biggest fright of his life in the final, when
the steering broke at 270 km/h. The Maserati
brushed the barriers on the outside of the oval
and by some miracle, Moss managed to bring it to
a halt. The boss of Eldorado ice creams,
Mr. Zanetti, had it repaired and entered it in the
Indianapolis 500 Miles in 1959, without Moss as
he was tied up with a Grand Prix. Today, Stirling
regrets having missed out on an experience which
his father had savoured before him. It should be

added that, two weeks after this accident, not
in the slightest put off by Maseratis, he raced
in the Sports Grand Prix of Vila Real in Portugal
with a 300 S, winning the race, having taken
pole and the fastest race lap, beating Behra in
the other 300 S.

The ACF Grand Prix at Reims on 6th July was
marked by two events: the death of Luigi Musso,
who went off the road at the Gueux corner in his
Dino-Ferrari and the retirement of Fangio, for
whom this was his last race. An era had come to
an end. Mike Hawthorn won the event, his only
victory of the season and also set the lap record.
Moss' Vanwall was losing oil and lost second and
third gears, but he still managed to finish second
after Behra retired. Next stop, Silverstone.

On 19th July, the front row of the grid for
the British Grand Prix was split between four
marques: Vanwall first with Moss (1'39"4,) then
BRM with Harry Schell (1'39"8,) followed by
Cooper with Salvadori (1'40"0) and finally Ferrari

with Hawthorn (1'40"4.) But Peter Collins got the best start off the second row in his Ferrari, setting a ferocious pace. Moss was unable to keep up and on lap 25 the Vanwall broke a conrod. Collins won and Hawthorn was second again, setting a new lap record. Moss could see his chances of the championship seriously compromised. His win earlier that morning in the Sport race, at the wheel of a Lister-Jaguar did little to console him. Nor did a win the following day in the non-championship race at Caen, in a Cooper-Climax. In the German Grand Prix, on 3rd August, he had an ignition failure on the Vanwall, although he did set a new lap record. Vanwall won nevertheless, courtesy of Brooks. It was trying to keep up with Brooks which led to Peter Collins' death at the Nürburgring. Everyone loved Peter, a charming, generous man and an able and courageous driver. Collins had class. Moss and Hawthorn lost a very dear friend. Mike, who was closer to Peter than Stirling, was deeply affected by his death.

But the Championship carried on. On 24th August, the venue was Oporto, for the first Portuguese Grand Prix and Moss was determined to win. He took pole again, ahead of Hawthorn

• **96**_Silverstone, 19th July 1958: Archie Scott-Brown was a frequent winner in the Lister-Jaguar . Here, as a curtain raiser to the British Grand Prix, Moss won the Formula Sport race, having started from pole and set the race fastest lap. *(The Autocar Editorial)*

● **97**_Oporto, 24ᵗʰ August 1958: this Portuguese Grand Prix would have a significant effect on the outcome of the World Championship. Moss (Vanwall) lapped Mike Hawthorn (Ferrari Dino 256) and then let him un-lap himself.

● **98**_An unusual view of the Oporto circuit: in the Portuguese Grand Prix, Moss' Vanwall flies to another win. Note the straw bales, supposed to protect the cars from harder obstacles.

and Lewis-Evans. Moss led and this time his Vanwall held to the end. Hawthorn was a long way back and pitted to adjust his brakes. When he was back in the race, he drove flat out, braking the lap record. On the pit wall, Vanwall team boss, David Yorke, hung out a board for Moss which read "HAWTHORN-REC" (record.) Unfortunately, Stirling misread it as "REG" (regular.) Having passed Hawthorn, not long after he slowed and let Mike unlap himself. It would have been enough for Moss to cross the line to win. Maybe he was thinking back to the recent ACF Grand Prix at Reims, when Hawthorn, who was about to win, refused to lap Fangio. In this instance, Mike, who was ahead of Stirling, still had to complete a lap to finish second. On this lap, Mike spun and his Ferrari engine stalled. He tried to push start it, going the right way, but uphill. Moss came alongside on his slowing down lap and shouted out: *"Push it downhill. You'll never get it started like that!"* Hawthorn followed the friendly advice, got going again and saved his second place. But after the race, the stewards wanted to strip him of second place and the 6 points that went with

it, as Mike had travelled in the opposite direction to the circuit. It was Stirling who pleaded his friend's cause, with plenty of panache and facts to back it up. He pointed out to the officials that Mike was indeed going the wrong way, but on the verge and not on the track itself! This generosity of spirit, inconceivable in the modern era when champions are single minded in pursuit of titles, would cost him the championship. Apart from that, on 7th September at Monza, having again started from pole, ahead of Brooks, Hawthorn and Lewis-Evans, he retired with a broken gearbox on his Vanwall. Brooks won the Italian Grand Prix and Hawthorn was second yet again.

A Formula Sport interlude followed, which had everyone holding their breath. Moss raced an Aston Martin DBR1 in the Tourist Trophy at Goodwood on 13th September. He was teamed with Tony Brooks (who recounts the race for us,) winning the event by beating Jaguar, Lister-Jaguar and Porsche, in the absence of Ferrari, who had already wrapped up the Constructors' World Championship.

● **99**_At the end of the Portuguese Grand Prix, the first three finishers do a lap of honour in a Buick cabriolet: on the left, Stuart Lewis-Evans (3rd,) Mike Hawthorn on the right (2nd,) with Moss the winner.

The Formula 1 series would end in theatrical fashion in Casablanca on 19th October, when Moss still had a chance of becoming World Champion. To do it, he had to win the Grand Prix and set the fastest race lap, with Mike finishing lower than second. This time, Hawthorn took pole, ahead of Moss and Lewis-Evans. Nevertheless, Moss took the lead ahead of the excellent Phil Hill in the other Ferrari, Brooks and Hawthorn. On lap 30, Brooks retired the Vanwall and Phil Hill let Hawthorn pass. Moss understood what was going on: protected by Hill, Hawthorn only had to finish second ahead of the American and he would be sure of the title, even if Moss won the race and recorded the fastest lap. That was exactly what happened. This was bad enough for Stirling, who could have expected to be Fangio's natural successor after the Argentine retired. However, this irritation paled into insignificance as a drama unfolded. With twelve laps remaining the engine on Stuart Lewis-Evans Vanwall blew up suddenly, sending him into a spin and off the track. A fire broke out and the marshals took too long to deal with it and the 28 year old Englishman died from his burns a few days later, in hospital in London, where he was taken by plane. Vanwall were thus the first winners of the Formula 1 Constructors' Championship with 48 points, ahead of Ferrari on 40. Thanks to a fantastic job from Moss, Brooks and the late lamented Lewis-Evans, Tony Vandervell realised his dream of beating *"those bloody red cars."* But it was a painful victory and shortly afterwards, Vandervell announced that Vanwall was pulling out of racing for good.

Mike Hawthorn also announced his retirement from racing, having won the 1958 World Championship with 42 points, just one win, five second places and five lap records. He was killed in a road accident on 22nd January 1959. For

• **100**_Goodwood, 13th September 1958: in the Tourist Trophy, Moss prepares to take over the Aston Martin DBR 1 from Tony Brooks, going on to win the race.
(The Autocar Editorial)

(Photo Christian Bedei)

Tony Brooks:
"The best sports car driver in the world"

Friendship and respect were reciprocated between Moss and Brooks and still are. "The flying dentist" knew Moss well as a team-mate, not just in Formula 1 with Vanwall, but also in sports cars with Aston Martin:
"There was no number one driver in the Aston Martin team, even if one respected Stirling as probably the best sports car driver in the world. He followed team orders, but his influence on the management was also respected and therefore had an influence. I am sure Stirling was always concerned that he had handed over the car in good condition to his team-mate. That was the case in the Tourist Trophy, but he really tried to get the most out of it, in a methodical manner, so that if there was any potential weaknesses, they would come to the surface."

Moss, runner-up with 41 points, four wins, a second place and three lap records it was a bitter pill to swallow. He was decent enough to praise Hawthorn's achievement as the first Englishman to take the title, even if he always preferred wins on the track to post-season honours. In September 1989, interviewed by *Supercar Classics* on his 60th birthday, Moss cast his mind back to those days: *"If I had been World Champion, even six times, would that have meant I was better than Fangio? And if I hadn't, would that mean I was not as good as Hawthorn? I am happy the way I am, the one who should have been World Champion. That's more exclusive."* One takes consolation where one can. ∎

● **101**_Casablanca, 19th October 1958: first lap of the Moroccan Grand Prix. Moss (Vanwall) tussles with Phil Hill's Ferrari (no. 4,) who had already broken clear of Hawthorn's Ferrari and the rest of the pack.

Chapter *11*
1959
From front to back

Vanwall entered a few more events with Tony Brooks, but the heart wasn't in it, neither were the finances nor the technology. Moss was well aware that the future of the sport lay with the mid-engine configuration, but at the end of 1958, Ferrari and BRM both continued to trust in the front mounted engine. Aston Martin and the American Scarab were also preparing to come into Formula 1 with the same layout. The pretty Lotus 16, which looked like a "mini-Vanwall," did the same. Cooper was therefore Moss' only choice. For 1959, John Cooper continued with Jack Brabham, took on the American Masten Gregory and offered a drive to a young New Zealander, Bruce McLaren, who had won a "Driver to Europe" scholarship. Bruce McLaren, Cooper and Brabham were supported by Esso, while Moss stuck with BP. He retained his links with Rob Walker, who ran him in a Cooper T 51, with new Climax 2.5 litre engines. The four cyliinder FPF could only manage 240 horsepower, which was 40 down on the V6 Dino. However, Climax believed that on the majority of circuits, its torque, light weight and better drive would make up for the power deficit. The Cooper driver would soon prove that to be true, even though the Ferrari men, especially Tony Brooks, would defend their corner with honour.

• **102**_Monsanto, 23ʳᵈ August 1959: in the Portuguese Grand Prix, the Colotti gearbox on the Rob Walker team's Cooper-Climax held firm for once and Moss was back on the winning trail.

• **103**_Silverstone, 2ⁿᵈ May 1959: a new car to challenge the Ferrari 250 GT in a Grand Touring race: the Aston Martin DB4 GT with an aluminium body known as "Superleggera" Touring. Moss was the first to steer it to victory in the BRDC trophy.
(The Autocar Editorial)

• **104**_Monaco, 10ᵗʰ May 1959: the start of the Grand Prix on the straight along the port, between the Tabac corner and the Gasometer hairpin. Moss (Cooper no. 30) started from pole and with Behra (no. 46) had already pulled away from Brabham's Cooper (no. 14.)

After getting back into the racing groove by winning the New Zealand Grand Prix final at Ardmore, in the old 2.2 litre Cooper and then swinging by Sebring to compete in a Lister-Jaguar in the 12 Hours, he had his first encounter with a 2.5 litre Cooper, built in Dorking by Alf Francis, which was lent to him for the Glover Trophy at Goodwood on 30th March. He celebrated the new union by winning this first race and setting the fastest lap. But it had not been easy. Walker's Cooper only had single rear wishbones, whereas the factory cars had a double wishbone arrangement. According to Jack Brabham, who knew what he was talking about, this lessened the car's tendency to oversteer. A further problem was that John Cooper could only supply Rob Walker with the 4 speed gearbox, originally based on a Citroen box and modified by E.R.S.A. While they had worked miracles with the 2.2 litre Climax engines, how would they cope with the torque of the 2.5 litre units? Moss and Alf Francis turned to the Italian, Valerio Colotti, who had just set up the Tec-Mec company in Modena. He built them a box which would see a lot of ink devoted

to it, while it also leaked a lot of oil! A first test was carried out at Aintree, in the 200 Miles, where Moss raced a Cooper fitted with a BRM engine. He was leading until a bolt in the gearbox primary shaft let go and he could no longer select any gears. The Cooper-BRM was fixed and taken as a spare car to the Monaco Grand Prix, but it was the Cooper-Climax which was used in the end. At Monaco, on 10ᵗʰ May, half the sixteen cars on the grid were rear-engined. Moss was on pole (1'39" 6,) ahead of Behra, fresh from his Ferrari dowin at aintree and Brabham in the first of the factory Coopers. Behra led the first 22 laps ahead of Moss and Brabham. The the Ferrari engine began to falter and Moss took the lead. When Behra retired, Jack Brabham was second, but unfortunately, the Cooper's Colotti gearbox broke. Moss was yet again robbed of an almost certain win and, after driving a good race, Jack Brabham took his first World Championship Grand Prix win. The sidelined Moss also had to cope with watching his old friend Tony Brooks come second in a Ferrari, while Maurice Trintignant was third in the other Rob Walker Cooper.

P. RÉNARD

Designer: Owen Maddock

Engine
Make/type: Coventry-Climax FPF
Number of cylinders/configuration: 4 in line/rear-central
Capacity: 2490 cc
Bore x stroke: 94 x 89.9 mm
Compression ratio: 11.5:1
Maximum power: 240 horsepower
Maximum revs: 6750 rpm
Block material: alloy
Carburettors: 2 Weber twin-bodied
Valve drive: 2 overhead cams
Number of valves per cylinder: 2
Ignition: distributor

Transmission
Gearbox/number of gears: Colotti/5
Clutch: dry, single plate

Chassis
Type: multi-tubular structure
Suspensions: independent wishbones front and rear
Dampers: telescopic, helical springs
Wheels: 500 X 15 (front) / 650 X 15 (rear)
Tyres: Dunlop
Brakes: discs front and rear

Dimensions
Wheelbase: 2250 mm
Width: 1280 mm (front) / 1320 mm (rear)
Dry weight: 430 kg
Fuel capacity: 150 litres

Used from Monaco to Holland, then from Germany to
United States (1959) and in Argentina (1960).

• 105_In the Monaco Grand
Prix, Stirling led for a long time
after Behra retired, until his
Colotti gearbox broke on the
Cooper, handing Brabham
the win.

However, Moss was now convinced the car was good enough to win, as Brabham had proved. Then it was off Zandvoort, which saw the debut of the Aston Martin DBR4, driven by Roy Salvadori and Carroll Shelby. They were beautiful, splendid even, as was the DBR1 Sport, but they were too heavy; effectively turning up a year too late. For the Dutch Grand Prix on 31st May, Rob Walker had got his hands on a double wishbone

rear suspension model for Moss. This time, it was Sweden's Joachim Bonnier in a BRM P25 who took pole, ahead of Brabham and Moss. No doubt with his fragile gearbox in mind, Stirling made such a prudent start that he was only eighth at the end of the opening lap, then sixth on lap 15. It was not his style. Ahead of him, there was a ferocious battle with Bonnier having to fend off a surprising Gregory, then another duel between

Rob Walker: the Colotti box

Rob Walker, who died in the spring of 2002, was the last privateer entrant to win a Formula 1 Grand Prix: the 1968 British Grand Prix, with Jo Siffert in a Lotus 49. He spoke to us in 2001 for the magazine *"Automobile Historique,"* recalling the pivotal role Stirling Moss played in the history of his team and the equally important role of the Colotti box in its misadventures in the 1950 World Championship. *"The Colotti box was more his idea than mine. It was a marvellous box to use as you could change gear without the clutch. Unfortunately, it was badly put together and the measurements were incorrect. It was entirely the fault of those Italians at Colotti. It took them a while to work it out. If we had the right measurements from the start, we would not have had those countless breakages and we would have won the World Championship, probably three years in a row. After that, as we know, the Colotti box was fitted to the majority of racing cars.*

"After Moss' accident in 1962, I didn't replace him, because I paid him more attention than I did the races. I spent more time with him than with the cars. I had no intention of becoming a constructor and I was happy as a private entrant. For me, it was marvellous to have a driver that one really respects and it was a wonderful life. With someone like Stirling there was always a lot of tension, because if he did not win a race, the whole world knew it was our fault, not his, as he was the best driver at the time. Later, I had a lot of respect for Joseph Siffert. The difference between Jo and Stirling was that Stirling taught me a lot about racing and I passed that on to Siffert. So in some ways, I put more of myself into that time."

• 106_Rob Walker and
Stirling Moss: first and
foremost a great friendship.

Brooks and Brabham: two Coopers each hounding a BRM and a Ferrari respectively. It was only on lap 35, when he passed Gregory, that Moss got into the top three, behind Bonnier and Brabham. On lap 40, having dealt with Brabham, he closed on Bonnier. On lap 60, he took the lead but with 15 laps to go, it was all over when the gearbox broke yet again. What had happened? In Monaco, bolts holding the crown-wheel were too close to the gearbox casing and had broken and in turn smashed the pinions. This time it was the clutch arm. Rob Walker offered to release Moss from his contract until the Colotti boxes were revised.

The result of this arrangement was that for the next two Grands Prix, Moss found himself at the wheel of a pale green BRM P25, run by the British Racing Partnership or BRP Racing Team, set up by his father Alfred, in association with Ken Gregory, his manager.

In the meantime, his spirits were raised by another exploit in an endurance race. This year, unlike in 1958, Aston Martin had not planned to contest the entire Constructors' World Championship for Sports Cars, only taking part in the Le Mans 24 Hours. Moss convinced Reg Parnell to send the spare DBR1 to the Nürburgring 1000 Kilometres, where it had a good chance of winning. He told us how he did it. *"I said to him, 'listen, if we don't win I'll pay the costs.' Given that I'm quite mean, that said it all."* There was further motivation for the driver, as he had reached an agreement with Parnell, that if he won he would keep the prize money! In the end, Aston Martin sent two mechanics with the car, but all other expenses were paid for by Moss, who chose Jack Fairman as his team-mate. Jack, whom he had known at Jaguar, was not very quick, but he was reliable. He agreed to do no more than

• **107**_Modena Autodrome, May 1959: another first in sports cars: Moss would take the 2 litre Maserati Tipo 60, the multi-tubular "birdcage" to victory. Here, Stirling carries out the test of the very first prototype to leave the factory. *(The Autocar Editorial)*

• **108**_Nürburgring, 7ᵗʰ June 1959: the Aston Martin DBR 1 of Moss/Fairman on the Eifel, heading for another important win in the 1000 Kilometres.

• **109-110**_The key moment in the Nürburgring 1000 Kilometres: Jack Fairman brings the bent DBR 1 back to the pits, having gone off the track, watched by Stirling Moss. They talk briefly as Moss jumps in the cockpit while Fairman gets out.

the minimum amount of laps demanded by the regulations, leaving the bulk of the driving to Moss. In qualifying, with a 3.74 final drive, pulling 6000 rpm, Moss lapped in 9'43"1, Fairman in 10'16." The Behra/Brooks Ferrari was 4.6 seconds quicker but Moss was still confident. On 7ᵗʰ June, in front of 200,000 spectators, Moss drove one of his best races, adding to the legend of the Nürburgring. He shot out of the white circle like a Jack in the Box and was the first to the cockpit and away. His first lap, from a standing start, took 10'17." On his second lap, he already had a 19 second lead over Dan Gurney's Ferrari. In 17 laps, he beat his own lap record from the previous year sixteen times, getting down to 9'32"! When he stopped to hand over to Fairman, the Aston had a 6'30" lead over the second placed Porsche of Edgar Barth, who was ahead of the Ferraris of Allison (who had taken over from Gurney,) Gendebien (who had taken over from

Phil Hill) and Behra (who had taken over from Brooks.) Fairman did what he could but then the rain came. The Ferraris passed the Porsche and were closing on the Aston. In his 6ᵗʰ lap (the 23ʳᵈ of the race,) Fairman was hit by an out of control car and the Aston went off the road. It was only slightly bent, but the back end had fallen in a ditch, with the front end pointing up in the air. With a Herculean effort, the brave Fairman managed to get it back on its four wheels and onto the track. He returned to the pits several minutes after the Ferraris of Gendebien and Behra had passed by into a comfortable lead. Moss thought that all was lost and had put his helmet and goggles in his bag when he heard a shout of *"he's coming in!"* from his pits. He barely had time to get his helmet and goggles back on before rushing to jump into the Aston cockpit almost before Fairman had got out. He was now 1'10" down on the Ferraris. Moss drove like a man

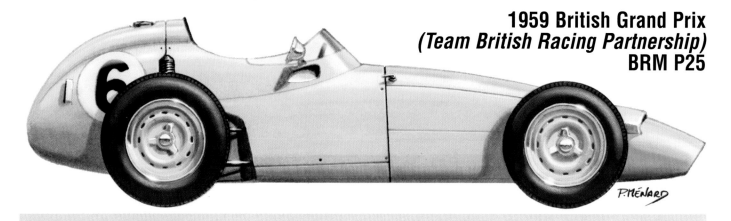

1959 British Grand Prix
(Team British Racing Partnership)
BRM P25

Designer: Tony Rudd

Engine
Make/type: BRM/P 25
Number of cylinders/configuration: 4 in line (front)
Capacity: 2491 cc
Bore x stroke: 102.9 x 84.9 mm
Compression ratio: 10.8:1
Maximum power: 278 horsepower
Maximum revs: 7800 rpm
Block material: alloy
Carburettors: 2 twin-bodied
Valve drive: 2 overhead cams
Number of valves per cylinder: 2
Ignition: magneto

Transmission
Gearbox/number of gears: BRM/5
Clutch: dry, single plate

Chassis
Type: tubular
Suspensions: independents (front and rear)
Dampers: telescopic, helical springs
Wheels: 600 X 16
Tyres: Dunlop
Brakes: discs front and rear

Dimensions
Wheelbase: 2320 mm
Width: 1320 mm (front) / 1280 mm (rear)
Dry weight: 550 kg
Fuel capacity: 180 litres

Used in ACF and in Great Britain.

● **112**_(Photo bottom right)
Aintree, 18th July 1959: in the
British Grand Prix, won by Jack
Brabham in the Cooper-Climax,
Moss is seen in the BRM P25
fighting with the young Bruce
McLaren. In the second works
Cooper, the New Zealander
finished 3rd right behind Moss.
(The Autocar Editorial)

possessed to close the gap in what is now a legendary drive. On lap 29, he had got the lead back from the Ferraris and on lap 33, he had extended it to two minutes. Fairman got back in for two laps, showing extreme caution. They were second again, 22 seconds off Gendebien's Ferrari, when Moss got in again for the final nine laps. He won by 41 seconds from the Gendebien/Hill Ferrari, in conditions which he adored. *"It was Aston Martin's third consecutive win in the Nürburgring 1000 Km. They were the only British company to have won this great German endurance classic and it was the sort of race I like best: a green and solitary Aston against the entire team of red factory Ferraris."*

In the Le Mans 24 Hours on 20th June, Moss and Fairman were again teamed together in one of the three DBR1s prepared by Aston Martin. The two others were driven by Roy Salvadori/Carroll Shelby and Maurice Trintignant/Paul Frere. Yet, again, Moss made a demon start and led for the first hour of the race. Jean Behra was pumped up in front of his home crowd and passed him, with Moss staying tucked in behind, benefiting from

the slipstream. Fairman took over, then one lap into his next stint, Moss was out thanks to a broken valve, caused by a fault in the engine cooling system. But Moss' drive had served to weaken the Ferraris and, on Sunday at 4 pm, the two surviving DBR1s took a brilliant one-two finish; Salvadori/Shelby ahead of Trintignant/Frere. This result meant that Aston Martin was now very much the main challenger to Ferrari in the Constructors' World Championship.

At Reims on 5th July, for the ACF Grand Prix, Moss met up with all his old friends: Trintignant (Rob Walker's Cooper-Climax,) Salvadori (Cooper-Maserati) and no less than five works Ferrari drivers: Jean Behra, Tony Brooks, Olivier Gendebien, Dan Gurney and Phil Hill – a record of sorts! Moss was racing a BRM P25. Outpaced in qualifying by Brooks, Brabham and Phil Hill, he started on the second row alongside Behra. In Brooks' slipstream, he managed to run second in the early stages, but he was then passed by Hill, Trintignant and Brabham. On lap 40, Moss passed Brabham and was attacking Hill when, braking for

Thillois, his BRM complete with broken clutch, went into a slide on the melting asphalt. The engine stalled. In suffocating heat of over 40 degrees, the driver tried to bump start it. He did not succeed and collapsed, almost fainting at the side of the track. Retirement was inevitable. He took consolation from setting the lap record in 2'22"8 at an average of 209.287 km/h and the point that went with it. Brooks had again driven magnificently to win the Grand Prix ahead of team-mate Phil Hill, followed by Jack Brabham.

Formula 2 was proving more successful for Moss at this time and, after Syracuse in April, he won the Coupe Internationale de Vitesse at Reims, on the day of the ACF Grand Prix. He repeated the feat the next Sunday at Rouen-les-Essarts, again in a Rob Walker Cooper-Borgward. Thanks to the excellent 1500 cc 4 cylinder Borgward, fitted to the Formula 2 Cooper, he took another win at Charade on 26th July. Eight days earlier at Aintree in the British Grand Prix, Moss in a BRM fought hard to finish second behind

• **111**_Reims, 5th July 1959: in the French Grand Prix, a heroic Moss pushed the BRM P25 to the point of exhaustion under a blazing hot sun in the Champagne region in his efforts to bump start it. It was all in vain. He had to settle for the fastest race lap, which was worth a point.

Brabham's Cooper. Behind Moss came a very incisive Bruce McLaren in the other works Cooper, just three tenths down on the Englishman.

The German Grand Prix took place at Avus on 2nd August. The day before, Jean Behra, whom Moss held in high regard, was killed in the Formula Sport race. The Avus track was criticised by the drivers for being very dull to drive as well as being ridiculously dangerous. It consisted of two long straights down an autobahn with corners at each end, one of them banked with a brick surface. It was at this point that Behra skidded in the wet. In the Formula 1 race, Hans Herrmann, who had taken over the BRP BRM P25, rolled spectacularly at the other end of the circuit. He was incredibly lucky to walk away unhurt. Moss was driving Rob Walker's new Cooper, on which the Colotti gearbox problems had allegedly been solved. Unfortunately, it broke yet again on the second lap of the Grand Prix, run in two 30 lap legs. The Ferraris of Brooks and Gurney won.

Finally, Moss' luck changed in Portugal. This 23rd August on the Monsanto circuit, three Cooper-Climax occupied the front row of the grid: Moss ahead of Brabham and Gregory. This time, Moss made a cautious start behind the other two, before passing them on lap 2. Brabham went off the road chasing Moss who, incredibly, slowed as he passed the pits to shout out to John Cooper that the driver seemed alright. Moss raced on alone, outpacing his rivals with apparent ease, all the time treating his Colotti gearbox with extreme care. It held to the end and Moss took his first Grand Prix win of the season, having lapped the entire field, including Masten Gregory who would finish second, five laps from the flag. Added to the previous day's pole position, he also set the fastest lap. Moss had got the lot – perfection.

• 113_Berlin, 2nd August 1959: on the banked corner at Avus, with a brick surface where Jean Behra was killed the day before in a Formula Sport race. At the same spot, Moss' Cooper battles with Tony Brooks' Ferrari, which would win the Grand Prix after Moss retired in the first leg, with transmission failure.

● **114**_Monsanto, 23ʳᵈ August 1959: Moss has just won the Portuguese Grand Prix in Rob Walker's Cooper-Climax. But this victory, which he celebrates with gusto, came a bit too late in the season.
(Copyright Autosport)

At Monza, he again took pole, ahead of Tony Brooks' Ferrari and Brabham's Cooper. The three leaders of the 1959 championship were on the front row in championship order. Alf Francis had finally fitted wheels with one central nut, to make for quicker changes if necessary. Tony Brooks was out at the start with a cooked clutch. Moss found himself second behind Phil Hill's Ferrari and ahead of Brabham in the Cooper. As expected, the tyres on the Ferrari wore out quicker and Phil Hill had to pit for a change. Moss was now in the lead and drove carefully to conserve his tyres all the way to the flag. He had won the Italian Grand Prix ahead of Phil Hill's Ferrari and Brabham's Cooper. It was enough for Cooper to claim the Constructors' Cup ahead of Ferrari.

● **115**_Monza, 13ᵗʰ September 1959: it was a close fight between the Cooper-Climax and Dan Gurney's Ferrari in the Italian Grand Prix. Stirling went on to win and the American finished 4ᵗʰ.

● **116**_Sebring, 12th
December 1959: the start of the
first United States Grand Prix.
On the front row, the Cooper-
Climax of Moss (no. 7,)
Brabham (no. 8) and Schell
(no. 19.) McLaren went on to
win the race and Brabham was
crowned World Champion.

For Brooks, Brabham and Moss there was one more chance to take the Drivers' title. It would all hinge on the final race of the season, also the first in the United States at Sebring in Florida on 12th December. Moss had to beat Brabham and set the fastest lap. The two Rob Walker Coopers, for Moss and Trintignant, were fitted with the big valve Climax engines. On a circuit he knew well having raced in the sports car 12 Hours race, Stirling took pole ahead of Brabham and Schell, racing here with a Cooper-Climax. BRM was absent. Moss took control at the start and pulled out a lead, when on lap 6, his Colotti gearbox gave out yet again and his chances had evaporated. Brooks was unlucky to be eliminated in a collision which was the fault of his Ferrari team-mate, Von Trips. Bruce McLaren won the race. He was the revelation of the season and the youngest winner of a World Championship Grand Prix (22 years, three months

and twelve days) a record which stood until Fernando Alonso's win in Hungary in 2003. Behind him came Trintignant and Brooks. Brabham was delayed and came home fourth, but it was enough to take the title.

Aston Martin were also champions in 1959, taking the Constructors' Championship in sports cars. Yet again, Moss played a decisive role. After the Nürburgring 1000 Km, on 5th September, Stirling won the Tourist Trophy at Goodwood, in rather strange circumstances. After a lightning start in the DBR1 he came in to hand over to Roy Salvadori. But while it was being refuelled, the car and the pits caught fire! The fire was put out and Moss took over the other DBR1 from Jack Fairman, who was sharing it with Carroll Shelby. Moss closed on the leading Porsche, winning the race and enough points for Aston Martin to overtake Ferrari and Porsche in the final classification. ■

● **117**_Goodwood, 5th September 1959: a great shot of Moss in the Aston Martin DBR 1 at Goodwood, on his way to winning the Tourist Trophy, having taken over the Shelby/Fairman car. The one he was sharing with Brooks had caught fire during refuelling! Victory here brought Aston Martin the Constructors' World Championship for sports cars.

Chapter 12
1960
Missed opportunities

D uring the winter of 1959-60, Stirling's private life was running into trouble. His marriage to Katie Molson was not a happy one, each partner having different aspirations in life. Gradually, the relationship fell apart and the couple announced it was separating in March 1960. Stirling was once again a very eligible bachelor, with a full address book and a love of going out to dance clubs at night. But underneath it all, he was deeply troubled. He compensated for this by burying himself in his work. At the start of the season, still with Rob Walker, Moss was still racing a Cooper-Climax. On 9th January he took part in the New Zealand Grand Prix and on 7th February, he competed in the opening round of the World Championship, the Argentine Grand Prix at Buenos Aires. He took pole and the fastest race lap, but did not repeat his 1958 win. This time, the suspension broke on the Cooper and Moss took over Trintignant's car, which he brought home third. It should be noted that, as from this year, a driver taking over another's car was no longer eligible for points. Furthermore and a sad blow for Formula 1, the point which rewarded those chargers who set the fastest race lap, was no longer awarded.

● **118**_Monaco, 29th May 1960: after Cooper, Lotus became the marque of the future for Formula 1. Here again, Moss was the first to take it to victory in the shape of this 18 with a Climax engine, entered by Rob Walker for the Monaco Grand Prix.

• **119**_Sebring, 26ᵗʰ March 1960: the Moss-Gurney Maserati "Birdcage" leads at the start of the 12 Hours. It retired with transmission failure.

Before tackling the World Championship, Moss drove in sports car races with a Maserati Tipo 61, belonging to the Camoradi team and in Formula 2, with a Porsche lent to Rob Walker by the factory. Moss loved the Maserati "birdcage" Tipo 61 with its 6 cylinder 2890 cc engine putting out 250 hp and a generous amount of torque. It

was very light (600 kg,) fast, with impeccable manners and very good brakes. In this car, he won the Cuba Grand Prix at Havana, retired in the Sebring 12 Hours and took yet another superb victory in the Nürburgring 1000 Km, in the rain and fog, partly due to a decisive stint from a very brilliant team-mate, Dan Gurney.

• **120**_Syracuse, 29ᵗʰ March 1960: after the Cooper-Borgward, Moss drove this Rob Walker Porsche in Formula 2. Having taken pole, the lap record and led the race, Moss retired. But he took the Porsche to victory in Brussels, Aintree, Zeltweg and East London. Note how near the spectators are to the track.
(The Autocar Editorial)

But the big novelty in this month of May 1960 was Rob Walker's acquisition of a Lotus 18 to replace Moss' Cooper. In April, he had been beaten by a factory version of this car by Innes Ireland at Goodwood. The Scotsman added salt to the wounds in May at Silverstone, taking another win and the lap record. Moss explained: *"That day, I followed him for 37 laps and I could see that the Lotus 18 had better drive and that it also had better corner speed."* The Lotus 18 was delivered to Rob Walker a few days after this BRDC Trophy at Silverstone. Moss was deeply impressed when he tried it for the first time at a private test at Goodwood. He remarked on how easy it was to drive and commented that the car was *"an extension of the driver."* However, he discovered that there were so many subtle permutations when

it came to adjusting the set-up and suspension that it was rather complicated. The Lotuses were engineers' cars. For the Monaco Grand Prix on 29th May, the Rob Walker team brought both the Cooper and the Lotus. Having delivered an eloquent comparison after first practice, Moss chose the Lotus, despite his concerns about its strength, particularly in terms of suspension and steering. In Buenos Aires, Ireland's 18 *"fell to bits,"* according to Stirling after a scintillating start to the race. Sadly, his concerns were not unfounded. The Lotus was the result of its creator's obsession with reducing unsprung weight. Colin Chapman is well known for saying that, *"the perfect race car is one that falls to bits as it crosses the line to win the race."* The annoying thing was that the Lotus would often break BEFORE the line.

● **121**_Nürburgring, 22nd May 1960: Moss was unbeatable at the wheel of the Camoradi team 2.9 litre Maserati Tipo 61 Birdcage in the Nürburgring 1000 Kilometres, which he won for a fourth time, (the third in a row,) this time with a co-driver who was almost as quick as him; Dan Gurney.

Nevertheless, at Monaco, Moss took pole in this brand new Lotus in 1'36"3, ahead of the Coopers of Jack Brabham (1'37"3) and the young British hope Chris Bristow (1'37"7.) At the start of the race, Moss followed Brabham and Bonnier, in the new rear-engined BRM. He tried not to ask too much of the Lotus, for fear of breaking it. This cautious approach was not his style but it would pay off. It began to rain and Brabham retired having crashed out at Sainte-Devote. Bonnier was delayed and despite having to pit to have a plug lead refitted, Moss won the race ahead of Bruce McLaren. The young New Zealander, who had won in Argentina, was now leading the world championship classification. In this race he also

beat the lap record. Moss' win was also a great success for Rob Walker's team and, for Lotus it was a first win in a world championship event from the team which had delivered the same for Cooper in Argentina in 1958. At the Dutch Grand Prix at Zandvoort on 6th June, Moss again started from pole. Ireland's works Lotus was also on the front row, with Brabham's Cooper in between them. As expected, Brabham led from the start and as in Monaco, Moss who had grown tired of criticism in some quarters of the British media that he was a car breaker, was following along quietly in second. Unlike in Monaco, it did not pay off. Brabham rode a kerb going through a corner. He dislodged a piece of concrete which came to

Lotus 18-Climax
(Team Walker)
1960 United States Grand Prix

P. MÉNARD

Designer: Colin Chapman

Engine
Make/type: Coventry-Climax FPF Mk II
Number of cylinders/configuration: 4 in line/
rear-central
Capacity: 2490 cc
Bore x stroke: 94 x 89.9 mm
Compression ratio: 11.5:1
Maximum power: 240 horsepower
Maximum revs: 6750 rpm
Block material: alloy
Carburettors: 2 twin-bodied
Valve drive: 2 overhead cams
Number of valves per cylinder: 2
Ignition: distributor

Transmission
Gearbox/number of gears: Lotus*/5
Clutch: dry, single plate
*Colotti after Monaco

Chassis
Type: multi-tubular structure
Suspensions: independent double wishbone,
front and rear
Dampers: telescopic, helical springs
Wheels: 5.50 x 15 (front) / 6.50 x 15 (rear)
Tyres: Dunlop
Brakes: discs front and rear

Dimensions
Wheelbase:
Width:
Dry weight: 410 kg
Fuel capacity: 150 litres

Used in Monaco and in Holland and from Portugal to
United States.

rest in one of the front tyres on the Lotus. Moss pitted to change it and rejoined twelfth and last but one. This left him no choice but to attack all the way to the finish, which he reached in fourth place, 1.1 second behind third placed Graham Hill in a BRM. The championship fight was on again, with Moss on 11 points behind McLaren on 14 and ahead of Brabham on 8.

Stirling now changed tack and decided that the best way to win was from the front, rushing away from the start and pulling out a big lead; a style later adopted by Jim Clark and much later by Ayrton Senna.

The tactic did not work in the Belgian Grand Prix at Spa. It was a black weekend which claimed the lives of Chris Bristow and Alan Stacey. Moss was lucky to escape with his life, after a spectacular accident in practice on Saturday 18th June. He was coming down the descent at Burnenville in 5th gear at 225 km/h, when he went over a bump and felt the Lotus go out of control. A rear wheel had come off. After braking as hard as he could, he spun and the driver prepared himself to crash backwards into a barrier. He was injured, with blurred vision and multiple fractures, but he was conscious. He was taken to hospital in Malmedy and then two days later transferred to London. Intensive physio followed and Moss was back in the cockpit less than two months later, on 7th August at Karlskoga

● **122**_Monaco, 29th May 1960: the first lap of the Grand Prix, at the Gasometer hairpin. Behind Bonnier's BRM and the Coopers, which have pulled away, can be seen Moss' Lotus (no. 28) on the apex. (*The Autocar Editorial*)

in Sweden, for a Formula Sport race, in an open Lotus 19 entered by the Yeoman Credit team. He celebrated his return with a victory, a first for this car and the fastest race lap.

The serious business kicked off again in Oporto with the Portuguese Grand Prix on 14th August. While Moss had his back turned, so to speak, Brabham had won the Belgian, French and British Grands Prix building up a lead in the world championship which would be hard to catch, even if drivers could only count their best six results. Bruce McLaren was second in Belgium,

third in France and 4th in the British and also had a good lead over Moss. Stirling had decided to give his all in this event, which also saw the World Championship debut of Jim Clark and a first F1 pole for world motorcycle champion John Surtees, driving a works Lotus 18. Moss was at the wheel of a new Rob Walker 18, fitted with a Colotti box. What was Moss thinking of? He explained that he preferred the action on the Colotti box with its classic shift pattern, to the Lotus box, with a lever that only moved forward and back, a bit like a modern sequential change.

● **123**_Monaco, 29th May 1960: on the podium after the finish, Moss is congratulated by Prince Rainier and Princess Grace of Monaco.
(The Autocar Editorial)

● **124**_Zandvoort, 6th June 1960: after the finish of the Dutch Grand Prix, Moss looks and laughs at the brick kicked up by Brabham's Cooper, which forced him to make an urgent pit stop!
(DR)

In the race, Moss battled with Surtees, who was pressing on so hard he went off the road. Moss was slowed with engine problems and had dropped to 10th when his engine stalled shortly before the finish. In a reprise of a previous race incident, he tried to bump start his car by pushing it against the direction of travel, downhill at the side of the track. It was exactly what he had advised Mike Hawthorn to do at the same track two years earlier. While Hawthorn had got away with it, this time the Portuguese stewards disqualified the culprit. In terms of the title, it did not really matter as no one, Moss included, could stop Brabham with his five consecutive wins from being crowned World Champion for the second year in a row.

The Italian Grand Prix, at Monza on 4th September was boycotted by the English teams, who were protesting against the decision of the Italian organisers to stage the race on a combination of the road circuit and the high speed track. This would favour the cars with the best top speed, namely the Ferraris. They won as they pleased, with Phil Hill, Ritchie Ginther and Willy Mairesse making it an all-red top three. It delighted the tifosi and it was also the last ever win for a front-engined car in the Formula 1 World Championship.

Last event on the calendar was the United States Grand Prix run at Riverside in California on 20th November. Moss was on pole yet again, ahead of Brabham and Gurney (BRM.) He went on to win, driving an exemplary race. He passed Brabham, who had led from the start on the second lap and was never seen again. Stirling won with a 38 second lead over Ireland and was left with regrets over a title which had slipped through his fingers.

● **126**_Riverside, 20th November 1960: a great win for Moss who had to fight for it in Rob Walker's Lotus 18, ahead of Innes Ireland's works car in the United States Grand Prix. It was run just once on the Californian track before heading to the East coast. (Photo Bernard Cahier)

● **125**_Oporto, 14th August 1960: in the Portuguese Grand Prix, Moss is seen here at the wheel of Rob Walker's Lotus-Climax. He would suffer an injustice and a humiliating disqualification.

The season did end on a positive note in other disciplines. In Formula 2, he won in Rob Walker's Porsche at Zeltweg in the Austrian Grand Prix and at East London in South Africa. In sports cars, after Karlskoga, Moss took the Lotus 19 (called the "Monte Carlo" as the intention was to beat the Cooper Monaco) to victory at Laguna Seca on 23rd October in the Pacific Grand Prix. This race carried big prize money and along with the Los Angeles Times Grand Prix at Riverside formed a series which would later give rise to the Can Am championship. In Grand Touring cars, he won the Tourist Trophy at Goodwood on 20th August. He was racing a short wheelbase Ferrari 250 GT, 2111 GT entered by Rob Walker. Moss recalled spending a quiet moment in the cockpit listening to the BBC broadcast of the race, interspersed with musical interludes, on the on-board radio while reeling off laps in the lead! ■

• **127**_Goodwood, 20th August 1960: the Tourist Trophy in this magnificent short wheelbase Ferrari 250 GT berlinetta, entered by Rob Walker. Moss had such a troublefree race that he was able to listen to the BBC commentary on the car radio. Note the aerial on the roof and how close the photographer is to his subject. *(Autocar Copyright)*

● **128**_Zandvoort, 22ⁿᵈ May 1961: Ginther's Ferrari leads the strongest threat to the Italian team: Stirling Moss in the Rob Walker Lotus 18. This Dutch Grand Prix was won by Von Trips (Ferrari.) Moss had to settle for fourth.

Chapter 13
1961
"Small" Formula, big wins

• **129**_Silverstone, 6th May 1961: Rob Walker's Cooper-Climax T53 "Intercontinental" brought Moss many wins and great moments such as here in the BRDC trophy, in a Formula which enjoyed great success in England after the introduction of the 1500 cc engine to F1. (*The Autocar Editorial*)

Over the winter of 1960-61, the English constructors were worried: the CSI (Commission Sportive Internationale) had confirmed a rule change for Formula 1, applicable from 1961. The maximum engine capacity is fixed at 1500 cc with a minimum weight of 450 kilos. Cars must also be fitted with a roll-over hoop and an electric starter. The English did not have a competitive 1500 cc engine. The Climax 4 cylinder FPF Mark II only put out around 150 horsepower. Coventry-Climax and BRM were working on V8s, but the former would not be ready until the summer of '61 and the latter at the start of 1962. Ferrari on the other hand had a powerful V6 (180 horsepower) and Porsche had a flat four, developed from Formula 2, which was not quite as strong, but would allow the German marque to come into Formula 1.

The English constructors lobbied the CSI for a long time to at least defer the decision, arguing lack of competitivity, prestige and spectacle if the Blue Riband of motor racing ran with such small engines. All they got for their troubles was the creation of a formula called "Intercontinental," where they could run engines up to 2.7 litres in non-championship events. These would be held mainly in Australia, New Zealand and England.

Moss made the most of the series, winning the Australian Grand Prix at Sydney's Warwick Farm circuit on 29th January in a 1960 Formula 1 Lotus 18. He also won the Lavant Cup at Goodwood on 3rd April and the International Trophy at Silverstone on 6th May, with the new Cooper 2.5, which Rob Walker had acquired to contest the Intercontinental Formula.

It should be remembered that the 1952 and '53 World Championships were run with 2 litres F2 cars. Anyone who thought this would be Formula 1 "on the cheap" was proved wrong and the 1500 cc Formula 1, which ran to the end of 1965 would also provide a thrilling contest. It would give rise to a whole new breed of drivers, such as Jim Clark, Graham Hill and John Surtees and a new extremely fast and sophisticated type of car, such as the BRM V8, Lotus 25, Ferrari (156, 158 and 1512) and the Honda transverse V12. The side effect of all this technology was that the private teams would have trouble competing at the highest level. But in 1961, Rob Walker and Stirling Moss would still stir things up, despite an obvious technical handicap. This applied not only to the engines, but also to the chassis. Lotus brought out a new model, the 21, which was only available to the factory drivers, Jim Clark and

Innes Ireland. Why? Because Team Lotus was sponsored by Esso, while Walker and Moss were backed by BP. Esso forbade Colin Chapman to sell a 21 to Walker. Stirling had to make do with a 1960 18, fitted with a 1.5 litre Climax FPF. The season got off to a mediocre start, because of recurring carburation problems later solved by Alf Francis. Stirling could do no better than fourth in the Glover Trophy, seventh at Heysel in the Brussels Grand Prix and eighth at Syracuse. This last event was won by the young Italian, Giancarlo Baghetti in a Ferrari 156. Moss was seriously worried about Monaco.

However, the race in the Principality would deliver one of his most sensational wins. A new Climax, the FPF Mk II, was put at his disposal,

• **130**_Monaco, 14th May 1961: along with the German Grand Prix the same year, this race saw Moss at the highpoint of his career. In Rob Walker's Lotus 18 (note the missing bodywork to improve cooling, and reduce weight) he demolished the opposition, especially Ferrari.

with a stronger bottom end producing slightly more torque and a few more revs. Moss took pole position ahead Ginther's Ferrari and Clark's Lotus. On the grid, Alf Francis noticed that one of the chassis tubes on the Lotus was cracked. With no time to empty and refill the fuel tanks, Alf proceeded to weld up the damaged pipe, having previously placed a few damp rags around the carburettors! Moss was determined to show the Ferrari drivers a thing or two. Ritchie Ginther was on form that day and took the lead, but Moss tucked in behind and relieved him of it on lap 14, with Bonnier's Porsche following him through. After a bad start, Hill in the other Ferrari closed the gap. He passed Ginther then Bonnier and started pressuring Moss, still in the lead. The two American Ferrari drivers began to give Moss a hard time, while Von Trips in the third Ferrari was lying fifth. Ginther's lap times came down consistently and he passed Hill, who would finish third and stuck like glue to Moss. His quickest lap was a 1'36"3, with Moss equalling that time on lap 85. Ginther never let up and finished second

just 3.6 seconds down on Moss, who had produced one of his best ever races in conditions which he loved: down on power, in a privately entered English car, out on his own on a track where the driver input is at its highest and beating the Ferraris on the way! At Zandvoort, on 22nd May in the Dutch Grand Prix, it looked as though it was too much to ask of Moss' old Lotus 18. This time, he had to give best to the Ferraris of Von Trips, recording his first grand prix win and Hill, as well as Jim Clark's Lotus 21. Moss just managed to hang on to fourth place, one tenth of a second ahead of Ginther. Then, on 18th June on the super-fast Spa-Francorchamps circuit, the Belgian Grand Prix turned into a display of Ferrari power, with the red cars filling all four top places, in the order, Hill, Von Trips, Ginther and Gendebien. Rob Walker's Lotus 18 had been modified with more fluid body lines and the rear suspension off the 21. Despite this, Moss, who might have been thinking back to his roll here in 1960, could do no better than eighth. At Reims for the ACF Grand Prix on 2nd July, the fight

• **131**_In Rob Walker's Lotus 18/21, Stirling seems concerned, during practice for the French Grand Prix at Reims. (*Photo* Christian Moity)

Designer: Colin Chapman*

Engine

Make/type: Coventry-Climax FPF
Number of cylinders/configuration: 4 in line/rear-central
Capacity: 1496 cc
Bore x stroke: 81.8 x 71.1 mm
Compression ratio: 9.5:1
Maximum power: 155 horsepower
Maximum revs: 7000 rpm
Block material: alloy
Carburettors: Weber twin-bodied
Valve drive: 2 overhead cams
Number of valves per cylinder: 2
Ignition: distributor

Transmission

Gearbox/number of gears: Colotti/5
Clutch: dry, single plate

Chassis

Type: multi-tubular structure
Suspensions: independent double wishbone, front and rear
Dampers: telescopic, helical springs
Wheels: 16"
Tyres: Dunlop
Brakes: discs front and rear

Dimensions

Wheelbase: 2250 mm
Width: 1280 mm (front) / 1320 mm (rear)
Dry weight: 460 kg
Fuel capacity: 130 litres

Used from Belgium to United States.

* This car is a Lotus 18, upgraded to 21 specification (bodywork, rear suspension) by Alf Francis for Rob Walker.

in the heat and debris proved Moss' undoing, just as it did for the Scuderia drivers. Stirling had to stop twice to have a brake caliper checked, as it was rubbing having collected molten tar. Rejoining, he was following Phil Hill closely when the American spun at Thillois because of the melting surface and the ensuing collision was inevitable. The carnage meant that an unexpected victory came the way of Baghetti, making his world championship debut in a Ferrari 65 degree 156, lent to the Scuderia Sant'Ambroeus. The Italian did a great job holding off Dan Gurney's Porsche as the race reached a thrilling climax.

At the British Grand Prix, staged at Aintree on 15th July, everything fell back into place for the factory Ferraris. This time, Von Trips beat Hill and Ginther. But rain at the start of the race meant that Moss was able to keep up with the lead group. On lap 24, he skidded on the wet track, caught it and having lost just ten seconds, set off again in pursuit of Ginther. The rain stopped and

the track began to dry allowing the Ferraris to once again exploit their power advantage. A broken brake line forced Moss to stop. Given it was his home race, he could not bear to be relegated to the role of spectator, so he took over Jack Fairman's car, also entered by Rob Walker; a four wheel drive Ferguson-Climax P 99. However, he was disqualified for having been push started. Moss still gets in a rage today when recalling the incident: *"Jack Fairman had been helped with a push start in the early stages and the race officials turned a blind eye. The Ferguson was not well placed at the time. Maybe it was when they saw I had taken over at the wheel that they decided to announce the disqualification."* In the meantime, Von Trips had reinforced his challenge for the title, with 27 points to Hill's 25 and Ginther's 16. Moss only had 12. He would go great guns at the Nürburgring, as we will discover in the next chapter. "It was a memorable race."

• **132**_Watkins Glen, 8ᵗʰ
October 1961: at the start of
the United States Grand Prix,
which would be his last World
Championship event, Moss
(Lotus) chases Brabham
(Cooper.) The race was won
by Ireland (Lotus.)

The next stage in the World Championship
would be dramatic. As usual at the start of
September, drivers and teams found themselves in
Monza for the Italian Grand Prix. At the Beginning of
the race, a probable misunderstanding between
Von Trips and Jim Clark led to the Ferrari crashing
heavily, flying into the crowd and killing several
spectators. Von Trips was thrown from the cockpit
and died instantly. Phil Hill won the race to
become World Champion as the paddock
mourned its loss. The day before the race, Moss
tried Rob Walker's brand new V8 Climax, but it
was not properly sorted. He started in a works

Lotus 21 with a V8 Climax engine, generously lent
to him by Innes Ireland who, with few points in
the championship whereas Moss was still in with
a chance of troubling the Ferraris, drove Rob
Walker's 4 cylinder car, which was off the pace
here. It changed nothing as, while battling with
Gurney for second place behind Hill, the front left
hub on Moss' Lotus let go, worn out by the
strains of lapping on the high speed oval section.
That left just the United States Grand Prix
on 8ᵗʰ October at Watkins Glen as the final round
of the championship which had already been
decided. Having taken the Constructors' title,

Ferrari did not take part. Innes Ireland finally enjoyed the satisfaction of winning with the 21, which although not the first win for the marque, was the first victory for Team Lotus in a Grand Prix. Moss was yet again at the wheel of Rob Walker's 18/21 and led from the start, fighting with Brabham. No one knew it at the time, but this was Moss' 66th and last ever World Championship Grand Prix participation.

Fortunately for him and his fans, Stirling enjoyed and helped them enjoy many great moments in 1961. In non-championship Formula 1 events, he won Grands Prix in Denmark, Sweden, Vienna and Modena with the Lotus 18/21. More "exclusively" and therefore more to his liking, he won the Gold Cup at Oulton Park on 23rd September in the Ferguson P99. He

thus acquired the distinction of being the only man to ever win a race in a four wheel drive Formula 1 car. In Formula Intercontinental, with the Cooper, he took top honours in the British Empire Trophy in July at Silverstone. In sports cars, he staged two breathtaking demonstrations in a Porsche RS 60 at the Targa Florio and with an RS 61 in the Nürburgring 1000 Km; both times with Graham Hill as his co-driver. On both occasions he gave the Ferraris plenty to think about. He was leading the final stages of the Targa Florio when he was sidelined with a rare differential casing failure. He won again in a Lotus 19, in the Players 200 at Mosport on 24th June, taking the lap record on the way. He did it again at Laguna Seca, winning the Pacific Grand Prix after a thrilling dice with Dan Gurney.

• **133**_Before winning the Oulton Park Gold Cup on 23rd September 1961, the only win in Formula 1 for a 4 wheel drive car, Stirling Moss took over Jack Fairman's Ferguson-Climax P99 on 15th July at Aintree, in the British Grand Prix.

• **134**_The Madonia circuit, 30th April 1961: Moss loved the Targa Florio and its tortuous route. In the 1961 race, he shared this 2 litre Porsche Spider RS 60 with Graham Hill. They were leading, when 8 kilometres from the finish, the differential casing cracked and they were forced to retire.

• **135**_Goodwood, 3rd April 1961: Moss wins the Formula Sport Sussex Trophy in a 2.5 litre Lotus-Climax 19, entered by UDT-Laystall. In this car and at this circuit, on 1st May 1963, he tested his ability to drive after his convalescence.

Johnny Rives: "Moss is still the benchmark"

In the 1961 Le Mans 24 Hours, Stirling Moss was teamed up with Graham Hill in Rob Walker's Ferrari 250 GT, chassis 2735 GT, entered by Luigi Chinetti's N.A.R.T. team. As usual, Moss took the start. At the tenth hour, while lying third overall and leading the GT class, the beautiful Ferrari was forced to retire when a fan blade chopped through a water pipe. It was a beginner's mistake according to Moss, as the mechanics should have removed the fan before the start. Johnny Rives remembers it as though it was yesterday: *"Having seen Moss in action*

● **136**_Le Mans, 10ᵗʰ June 1961: Moss in Rob Walker's Ferrari 250 GT, chased by Roy Salvadori's Aston Martin on lap 2 of the 24 Hours, passing Walt Hansgen's Maserati Tipo 63 in the Dunlop curve a great moment.
(Editorial File Photograph)

for the first time in Monaco, I rediscovered his skill at Le Mans in 1961, watching him through the Dunlop curve, which was a delight in those days. He was in Rob Walker's navy blue 250 GT up against the two Aston Martins of Salvadori and Clark. They were all glued together and for two hours Moss controlled the situation perfectly. A bit later, it started to rain. You had to see Moss going through Dunlop with that Ferrari GT ahead of the two Aston Martins. I've seen a lot of races, but that scrap at Le Mans with Moss in the 250 GT and the two Astons, was a rare moment, a moment which cemented my love of motor sport. For me, Moss remains the benchmark, or at least after Fangio, who is still the absolute pinnacle. Fangio impressed me, but Moss seduced me. His car control was different to that of other drivers. I remember comparing Carlos Menditeguy driving the Maserati 250 F at Monaco in '57 with Moss' performance the previous year, when he got the very most out of the car. In April 1962, when he had his accident at Goodwood, me and my friend Bernard Gautier had to write up the news coming from the London hospital for "L'Equipe." It was a painful exercise as, at first, there were fears he would not survive. Then, when we knew he was on the road to recovery, the question was whether he would be able to race again."

And then there was the promise of Ferrari for 1962. The man from Maranello had made contact again with the British driver. A lot of water had run under the bridges of England and Italy since the affront of Bari in 1951. Enzo Ferrari was well aware of the odd occasion when the British champion had raced under the sign of the Prancing Horse, even if it had been with private teams such as Luigi Chinetti's NART or with Rob Walker. In fact, on 19ᵗʰ August, Moss had taken his seventh TT win at Goodwood, the second at the wheel of a 250 GT berlinetta. It was painted navy blue with a white stripe and was a "competizione" version, chassis 2735 GT. This time, he had won after a fierce battle with a young driver in another 250 GT, who had made a strong impression and would go on to join the Scuderia:

Mike Parkes. Moss won shorter races in this 250 GT, at Silverstone in July and Nassau in December. Not forgetting a great start to the Le Mans 24 Hours, which eye witnesses such as Johnny Rives remember to this day.

On 8ᵗʰ September at Monza, he tested an experimental prototype berlinetta, the future 250 GTO. Moss immediately recognised the potential of this extraordinary car and Enzo Ferrari promised delivery of the first customer version for the UDT-Laystall team, run by Ken Gregory and Alfred Moss; in other words for Stirling. The Commendatore also promised the Englishman a Formula 1 car, which according to his wishes would be run by Rob Walker in 1962. It was an exciting prospect, but sadly it was not to be. ■

Chapter 14
Fangio's successor

● **137**_Nürburgring, 6th August 1961: the last of Moss' 16 wins in the Formula 1 World Championship, in Germany in this Lotus-Climax 18, upgraded to 21 spec by Rob Walker. (The Autocar Editorial)

"A memorable race"

German Grand Prix 6th August 1961

On the eve of this Grand Prix, the three regular Ferrari drivers occupied the top three places in the championship classification: Germany's Wolfgang Von Trips had 27 points, to lead the Americans, Phil Hill (25) and Ritchie Ginther (16.) Stirling Moss was only fourth on 12 points. 26 cars qualified for this Grand Prix: two BRM P 48/57 with Climax engines, for Tony Brooks and Graham Hill: two Cooper-Climax T55 for Jack Brabham, the first to get his hands on the latest V8 Climax engine and Bruce McLaren: three Ferrari 156, 120 degree V6, 190 horsepower, for Von Trips, P. Hill and Ginther: another Ferrari 156, 65 degree V6, 180 horsepower for Belgium's Willy Mairesse; two Lotus-Climax 21s for Jim Clark and Innes Ireland; three Porsche RSK 718 (around 160 horsepower from a flat four,) for Joachim Bonnier, Dan Gurney and Hans Herrmann. That was the list of works cars. Added to these were the cars entered by private teams and drivers, of which there were still several in this era of Formula 1. First off of course was Rob Walker with the Lotus 18/21 for Stirling Moss; then the other Englishmen, Tony Marsh and Gerry Ashmore, the South African Tony Maggs and Germany's Wolfgang Seidel with Lotus-Climax 18; then Coopers for the Reg Parnell team (two T53-Climax for John Surtees and Roy Salvadori,) CAMORADI (a T 53 for Ian Burgess,) Centro-Sud (T 53 Maserati for young Italian hope Lorenzo Bandini,) SSS Serenissima (T 51-Maserati for France's Maurice Trintignant,) England's Jack Lewis (T 53-Climax) and Frenchman Bernard Collomb (T53-Climax.) Finally, in a private Porsche there was the Dutchman, Carel Godin de Beaufort. By a long way, Moss seemed like the only privateer who might be capable of beating the Ferraris here, as he had done in Monaco.

QUALIFYING

The big question in qualifying, apart from the usual ones about set-up and, in the case of the neophyte drivers, the difficulties posed in learning the track, was down to the choice of tyres. In his book *"My cars, my career,"* Moss revealed that, during qualifying, he had been impressed by the superior grip offered by the new Dunlop D12 rain tyres. On the down side, once the sun came out and the track dried and got hot, they would de-laminate. Moss decided to risk it, given that the weather forecast for Sunday was for rain. *"It was a calculated risk, which I had a feeling was our only chance against Ferrari, as Phil Hill had become the first man to lap in under 9 minutes."* One amusing detail: the Dunlop D12 tyres had a big green spot on the side and Rob Walker's team made a point of repainting them black to fool the opposition. In the end, Moss was the only driver to start on rain tyres!

STARTING GRID			
4. Bonnier 9:04.8	3. Moss 9:01.7	2. Brabham 9:01.4	**1. P. Hill 8:55.2**
	7. Gurney 9:06.6	6. G. Hill 9:06.4	5. Von Trips 9:05.5
11. Herrmann 9:12.7	10. Surtees 9:11.2	9. Brooks 9:09.3	8. Clark 9:08.1
	14. Ginther 9:16.6	13. Mairesse 9:15.9	12. McLaren 9:13.0
18. Lewis 9:31.4	17. De Beaufort 9:28.4	16. Ireland 9:22.9	15. Salvadori 9:22.0
	21. Trintignant 9:38.5	20. Marsh 9:37.7	19. Bandini 9:35.4
25. Ashmore 10:06.0	24. Burgees 10:01.4	23. Seidel 9:59.9	22. Maggs 9:45.5
		26. Collomb 10:23.0	

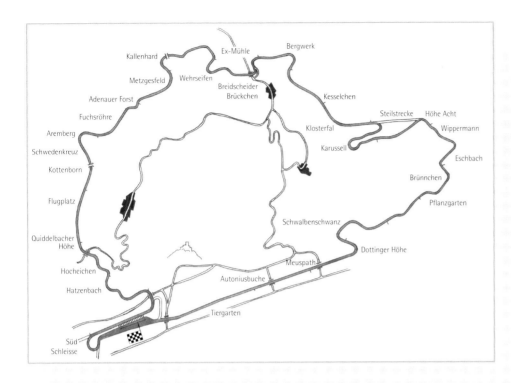

NÜRBURGRING, THE CIRCUIT
Permanent circuit,
22.810 km (north circuit)

Situated in the Eifel mountains in the Black Forest, in a grandiose setting around sixty kilometres to the south of Cologne, the Nürburgring circuit enjoys legendary status in the history of motor racing. Built from scratch in the Twenties, as part of a work creation scheme initiated by the Weimar Republic, it comprises two loops, the 22.810 km "Nordschleife" and the 7.7 km "Sudschleife." The latter was often used for motor cycle grands prix, while the North loop was the stage for the German Grand Prix, as well as the 1000 Kilometres race for Sports, Prototype and GT cars and a 24 Hour Touring Car race. In 1927, with a Mercedes SSK, Otto Merz was the first man to put his name in the record book. After that and in the pre-war years, it witnessed the brilliance of men like Caracciola, Chiron, Nuvolari, Rosemeyer, Lang and Seaman, while later it saw such stars as Ascari, Fangio, Moss, Clark, Stewart and Ickx leave their mark. It features 176 corners, vertiginous contour changes, dips and bumps which often saw cars fly through the air, a changing surface because of track deterioration and less than welcoming run-offs, making it impressive for drivers, constructors, mechanics and spectators alike. It was also a dangerous track where several famous drivers, including Peter Collins lost their lives. Drivers also had to contend with changeable weather; some parts remaining dry while others were wet or foggy and everything could change in the space of a lap. It was a fearsome challenge, for Moss and his peers on that day back in 1961.

● **139**_Just after the start of the German Grand Prix, Jack Brabham's Cooper-Climax (no. 1) has taken the lead ahead of Moss in the Lotus-Climax (no. 7,) Bonnier's Porsche (seen behind Brabham) and Phill Hill's Ferrari (no.4.)

● **140**_An exhausted but happy winner after a race where the rain was his ally.
(The Autocar Editorial)

THE RACE

It rained just before the start, but when Juan Manuel Fangio, winner here for the last and unforgettable time four years ago, lowered the flag, the track was dry, or at least it was in those areas which were not shaded. That was exactly what caught out Brabham, who had taken the lead from Moss, but went off a quarter of the way round the opening lap. Luckily, Jack was uninjured. Ireland also went off at the Carousel, as his Lotus caught fire. Innes also escaped injury. While this was going on, Moss had taken the lead, with a small advantage over P. Hill and Bonnier, who were locked in combat. In the heat of the moment, Bonnier hit the barrier and came in to change a wheel, while G. Hill retired after tangling with Gurney. Big Dan continued, but he was losing ground. Moss led P. Hill and Von Trips by 8"5 on the second lap and 11" on the fourth, which he covered in 9'13"5. On lap 7, Moss had increased his lead over the two Ferrari drivers, while Brooks and Bonnier had retired. Life could have been simple for the English driver, but for the fact the track was drying. On lap 10, the two Ferraris lapped in under nine minutes and had closed to within 10 seconds of Moss. He did his best to contain them, while trying to look after his ultra-soft tyres and hoping the rain would hurry back. Hill and Von Trips were wheel to wheel as they continued their all-Ferrari duel and had closed the gap to Moss to 6"5, when finally his prayers to the rain gods were answered! The ensuing downpour gave him an edge again and he crossed the finish line with just over 20 seconds in hand over Von Trips, closely followed by Phil Hill.

There are many who claim this was his greatest victory in a fabulous career. What is certain is that, sadly, it was his last ever win in the World Championship. ■

r Preis von Eu

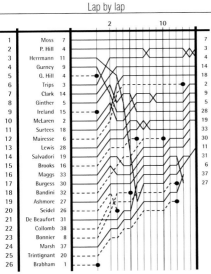

RESULTS - 15 racing laps or 342.150 km

1.	**Moss**	**Lotus-Climax**	**15**	**2:18:12.4**
				148.538 km/h
2.	Von Trips	Ferrari	15	+ 21.4
3.	P. Hill	Ferrari	15	+ 22.5
4.	Clark	Lotus-Climax	15	+ 1:17.1
5.	Surtees	Cooper-Climax	15	+ 1:54.1
6.	McLaren	Cooper-Climax	15	+ 2:41.4
7.	Gurney	Porsche	15	+ 3:22.6
8.	Ginther	Ferrari	15	+ 5:23.1
9.	Lewis	Cooper-Climax	15	+ 5:23.7
10.	Salvadori	Cooper-Climax	15	+ 12:11.5
11.	Maggs	Lotus-Climax	14	1 lap
12.	Burgess	Cooper-Climax	14	1 lap
13.	Herrmann	Porsche	14	1 lap
14.	De Beaufort	Porsche	14	1 lap
15.	Ashmore	Lotus-Climax	13	2 laps
16.	Collomb	Cooper-Climax	12	3 laps
17.	Marsh	Lotus-Climax	12	3 laps

RETIREMENTS

Mairesse	Ferrari	13	Accident
Collomb	Cooper-Climax	11	Disqualified
Trintignant	Cooper-Maserati	12	Engine
Bandini	Cooper-Maserati	10	Engine
Brooks	BRM	6	Valves
Bonnier	Porsche	5	Engine
Seidel	Lotus-Climax	3	Steering
Ireland	Lotus-Climax	1	Fire
G. Hill	BRM	1	Accident
Brabham	Cooper-Climax	0	Accident

FASTEST RACE LAP

P. Hill	Ferrari	8:57.8
		152.688 km/h

Lap by lap

_STIRLING MOSS' RECORD AT THE GERMAN GRAND PRIX

YEAR	CIRCUIT	QUALIFYING	FINISHING POSITION	CAR
1953	Nürburgring	12th	6th	Cooper-ALTA
1954	Nürburgring	3rd	Retired (con rod)	Maserati 250 F
1956	Nürburgring	4th	2nd	Maserati 250 F
1957	Nürburgring	7th	5th	Vanwall
1958	Nürburgring	3rd	Retired (magneto)	Vanwall
1959	Avus	2nd	Retired (gearbox)	Cooper-Climax
1961	Nürburgring	**Pole Position**	**1st**	Lotus-Climax

• **141**_Goodwood, 23ʳᵈ April 1962: Moss' last race, seen here on a charge at the wheel of Rob Walker's Lotus 18/21, run under the UDT Laystall banner.

Chapter 15
1962...
Goodwood
and beyond

The 1962 season got underway in the Antipodes. For the Tasman series, the Rob Walker team had shipped out a Formula Intercontinental Cooper T 53, fitted with a 2.7 litre Climax engine and the brand new Lotus 21 which Chapman had finally been allowed to supply to him. For the moment, it was fitted with a 2.5 litre, 4 cylinder Climax FPF engine. It was with this that Moss won the New Zealand Grand Prix at Ardmore, on 6th January in torrential rain. Once the 21 was back in Europe, Rob Walker planned to fit it with a new Climax V8, which would allow Moss to race it in Formula 1, if the promised Ferrari did not materialise.

For all the other Tasman series events, Moss abandoned the Lotus in favour of the Cooper. The final of the Vic Hudson Trophy at Levin was stopped because of pouring rain, much to Moss' annoyance, as he was about to pass Jack Brabham to take the lead. A week later in Christchurch, he won the Lady Wigram Trophy, then at Invercargill in the Teretonga Trophy, he finished second to Bruce McLaren, driving a similar car. On 4th February, in Australia this time, Moss started from pole and won the Warwick Farm 100 miles, near Sydney. It was his 212th win in an incredible career. No one, least of all the man himself, could know it would be his last.

A few days later, Moss was back in Florida, with a first appointment at Daytona. The famous circuit, near the beach which was the scene of several speed record attempts before the war, was made up of half the high speed oval and a flat road section in the infield. The Daytona Continental was run over three hours and open to

Grand Touring and Sports-Prototype cars. Moss had the good fortune to drive an excellent Ferrari; the experimental 250 GT berlinetta, chassis 2643 GT. Its beautiful bodywork, designed by Pininfarina, resembled the road-going "Superfast." Moss was using this while waiting for the promised delivery of the 250 GTO from the factory to the UDT-Laystall team. The race was won by Dan Gurney in a Lotus 19, ahead of the prototype Ferraris of Phil Hill and Ricardo Rodriguez, with Moss fourth overall and first GT. On 23rd March, still in Florida, the venue was Sebring for the Three Hours, for small capacity GT cars. As in the previous two years in the 4 Hours, Moss who did not turn his nose up at small cars, nor the start money, drove a factory-entered 997 cc Austin-Healey Sprite. He had finished second in 1960 behind a Fiat-Abarth and fourth in 1961, when other Sprites were driven by Bruce McLaren, Walt Hansgen and Pat Moss and this time, Moss finished third. At the start of the race, when it was raining, he led, but later the track dried and Hansgen and McLaren, in Fiat-Abarth's capable of 25 mph more than the Sprite, pulled away from him. Two days later it was time for more serious matters: the Sebring 12 Hours. For this event, Moss was at the wheel of a Ferrari 250 TR 61, the very same car which had won the Le Mans 24 Hours in the hands of Gendebien-P. Hill. It had been entrusted to the NART team of Luigi Chinetti, who was the marque's American importer. Unusually for a race with a "Le Mans" start, Moss let his team-mate Innes Ireland take the first stint. Running near the front, he was engaged in a dice with the Dino-Ferrari driven by the Rodriguez brothers. Then, Moss and Ireland

moved into the lead and their only worry would be pit stops to change brake pads, as the Testa Rossa had a healthy appetite in this area. But the NART team had entered eight cars. Consequently, it was chaos in the pits and they had forgotten to count the laps for each car. The two British drivers learnt, much to their annoyance that while leading and three hours after the infringement, they had been disqualified for stopping before completing twenty laps, as demanded by the rules! Back in Europe, Moss as

planned was back in Formula 1 mode. As Rob Walker's 21 had yet to return from Australia, the old 18/21 "special" was called into service, still in its navy blue livery, for the race in Brussels on 1st April. With this car, now resprayed in UDT-Laystall light green colours, under the management of Ken Gregory and Alfred Moss, Stirling took the final pole position of his career at Snetterton on the 14th. The race was a disappointment, with a seventh place finish, despite setting the fastest lap.

• **143**_Goodwood, Easter Monday, 23rd April 1962: a few seconds before the accident, approaching St. Mary's corner.

John Surtees: "Always a racer..."

"We had both been delayed by pit-stops in the early stages of the race, losing all chance of beating Graham Hill and the BRM for the win. But both of us were lapping quicker than him and it was while he was preparing to pass Graham that he had the accident which brought his career to a premature end. As far as I read the situation,

• **144**_Stirling Moss and John Surtees in 1988.

although Graham was not under pressure, he was certainly prepared to defend his lead. But he had not expected Stirling to catch him so quickly. On the approach to Saint Mary's, normally you would not move right over to the left of the track unless you were pushing very hard. I reckon Graham was on the usual line, nearer the middle of the track and he had simply not seen him. Stirling, always a racer, saw a gap on the left, but it disappeared when Graham cut across to take the right line going into the next right hander.
"I presume that Stirling then got his left wheels on the grass and that was it. I think that's what happened."

And then it was time for Goodwood on Easter Monday, 23ʳᵈ April. In the opening laps of the Glover Trophy, having started from pole, he was third behind Graham Hill's BRM and Bruce McLaren's Cooper. Then he was passed by John Surtees in the Lola-Climax. On lap 9, Moss pitted to have his gearchange adjusted. He rejoined in seventh place and immediately began to climb back through the field. Surtees had beaten the lap record in 1'23"0. Moss beat him by two tenths and both men were lapping in 1'22. What happened next has been described countless times, including at the start of this book. The exact cause of the accident remains a mystery. Moss himself remembers nothing about it. That is understandable given the violence of the impact and the injuries he sustained. John Surtees offers a plausible explanation for the accident in his autobiography "World Champion."

A few months later, after an arduous rehabilitation, Moss was able to walk and was recovering slowly. But he noticed that his eyesight had deteriorated as had his reflexes. At the same time as his physiotherapy programme under medical supervision, he also worked on sharpening his concentration with exercises like holding a pencil up against a sheet of paper. During this time, the fan letters piled up and his parents, who took turns to be with him, read him the innumerable goodwill messages. In the press, stories proliferated as to his chances of getting back behind the wheel and when that might happen, as well as going over the circumstances surrounding his accident.

It should not be forgotten that in 1962 Stirling Moss was a huge star at home and even on an international level. He was recognised in the streets of Paris, Milan, Buenos Aires and Vienna. It was around this time that a fan who had been at Goodwood at the exact spot where the accident occurred wrote to Alfred Moss. He said he had seen sparks coming from under the exhausts on Moss' Lotus, which made him think the car had passed over some debris, which although small, might have destabilised the car enough for Moss not to be able to control it when it began to go off the road. In short, it suggested that Moss' superior ability should not be brought into question. While such an eyewitness account might, even years later, pour balm onto the heart of an injured driver or those close to him, it also proves the limitations of trying to explain a racing accident, especially when the driver has died, as is the case with Ascari, Clark, Gilles Villeneuve and Senna. Although he was lucky enough to survive, it should be repeated that Moss has no recollection of the events of the accident, nor of the laps preceding it. He knew Goodwood like the back of

• **146**_A few weeks later, a bearded Stirling is recuperating as his friend Maurice Trintignant, who the day before Moss' accident at Goodwood, had won the Pau Grand Prix in Rob Walker's other Lotus pays a visit.
(Photo Bernard Cahier)

• **147**_Stirling Moss and Jim Clark (seen here in June 1961 before the Belgian Grand Prix.) The former would be forced into early retirement just as the latter was coming into his own. Formula 1 fans still dream of what their duels might have been like if Moss had not had his accident.

his hand and returned to the scene several times to try and understand. It was all in vain.

The only clear fact was that nothing would be the same again. After a few months, Stirling was well enough to resume normal daily life: reading, writing, eating and washing. In the Autumn of 1962, he returned to Saint Thomas' Hospital twice for corrective surgery, especially to his eye which had to be repositioned in its socket. He was delighted to find he was able to drive his Lotus Elite road car again. He took a few weeks holiday to convalesce in his home in the Bahamas. Of course, the grand prix season was going on without him and a bitter irony, it was his friend Graham Hill in a BRM who would be crowned World Champion, after a titanic tussle with Jim Clark and the Lotus 25. The young Scotsman was very much regarded as Moss' natural successor if the Englishman could no longer race, or his number one rival if he did return to the cockpit.

But there would be no return. Such was the pressure from the media, the fans, the constructors and team bosses that Moss accepted to have a private test, at Goodwood of course in the UDT-Laystall Lotus 19 Sport, with a Climax 2.5 litre engine. It took place on 1st May 1963. Ken Gregory and his chief mechanic Tony Robinson were in attendance. It had rained in the morning and the circuit was still wet in parts. The Lotus 19 was not exactly up to date. Moss drove for around half an hour with a best lap time of 1'39, three seconds slower than he felt would have been competitive. In 1986, at home in London, he

admitted to us that: *"with what it took to do those times, I knew that I would not be able to race. I had lost my concentration and in order to set these times I had to think about everything. Nothing came automatically. And when my powers of concentration returned, it was almost five years later, by which time everything about the sport had changed. Being out of action for a year or two is already a long time, but five years is really too much. And also, before that I was not scared to do what was needed. Afterwards, I was. And anyway, I had always thought I would retire if the day came when I was no longer the quickest."*

With hindsight, maybe the Goodwood test had come too early, as had the statement which Stirling had asked Ken to make back on that day in May 1963. In 1964, Ken Gregory relinquished his position as Stirling Moss' manager, going on to set up the BRP (British Racing Partnership) with Tony Robinson. They produced Formula 1 cars for Innes Ireland and Masten Gregory. Various projects for a return to racing had lost their importance for Stirling, who was now involved in other business activities, including property. Nevertheless he still dabbled in motor sport; first of all in 1964, setting up his own team S.M.A.R.T. (Stirling Moss Auto Racing team) which entered Porsche 904 GTS and Alfa Romeo GTZ "Tubolare." Then he became a race commentator for an American TV station. Thus the viewers saw a bearded Stirling, trackside, interviewing successive champions, from Jim Clark to Jackie Stewart, to Bruce McLaren and Jochen Rindt. He

also played an active role in the promotion of the Can-Am series up to 1974. He did actually race in Touring Cars with an Audi in 1980 and then in Historics. Stirling also collected, bought and sold a series of collectors cars over the year, from a Shelby Mustang to a Lola-Climax Mk 1, 1100 cc

and a Chevron B8, which he also raced in historic events as a gentleman driver, at tracks like Montlhery, Pau, Zolder and the Nürburgring. He was often invited as a guest of honour to retrospective events such as the Monaco Historic Grand Prix, the Festival of Speed and the Circuit

● **148**_Silverstone, March 1980: presentation of the Audi-Akai team with drivers, Richard Lloyd and a famous returnee, Stirling Moss. They would compete in the British Touring Car Championship in Audi 80 GLEs.

● **149**_Brands Hatch 1983: Stirling Moss in overalls, gloves, helmet and goggles in the fashion of the Sixties, gets behind the wheel of the turbocharged Brabham-BMW in which Nelson Piquet would win that year's World Championship: *"I wanted to experience the acceleration and braking of a modern F1 car. I was not disappointed!"*

Revival Meeting at Goodwood, events which have become an absolute must for the fans. Thus, we have seen him take to the track at the wheel of the Mercedes 300 SLR and W 196, Aston Martin DBR1, Maserati 250 F, Vanwall, Cooper-Climax, Lotus 18, Jaguar C type and Frazer Nash. He proved he was still a more than competent driver. His private life has also undergone many changes since the 1960s, even though he still lives in London in a West End house, done out with all the latest gadgets, giving it something of a James Bond aura. His second marriage in 1964,

to a beautiful American model, Elaine Barbarino, did not last too long. They had a daughter, Allison, in 1967 when they had already separated. Alfred Moss died of cancer in 1972, while Aileen survived him by eight years. A bachelor again in 1968, Stirling met up with the Paine family. He had know them in Hong-Kong when he was on his way to race in the Antipodes. In 1980, Susie, one of their two daughters would become Stirling Moss' third wife. Their son Elliot was born that year, with Jackie Stewart as godfather.

In the 2000 New Years Honours List, Stirling Moss was given a knighthood, receiving the accolade from Prince Charles at Buckingham Palace. Sir Stirling Moss is still a racer and leaves us to reflect on the concept of a racing driver's role in which he accepted all the consequences of success and failure: *"My philosophy about racing, which is not really shared today, is that it is very important to race while enjoying the sport. And I would prefer to lose a race driving quickly enough to have won it than to win by driving slow enough to lose it. Do you understand?"* ∎

● **151**_Brands Hatch, 3rd May 1987: Stirling and his son Elliot, then aged six, at an FIA Historic Championship meeting.

● **152**_London, 2000: in the final New Years Honours list of the twentieth century, Moss became Sir Stirling; Prince Charles bestowing the knighthood on behalf of the Queen.

_STATISTICS

In a career that began in 1948 and ended in 1962, Stirling Moss took part in 529 races (494 if one counts those that were run over 2 legs as a single event.) He won 212 of them. On top of that there were numerous trials, hill-climbs, rallies and record attempts, which added up to over 50 starts. The races were in Formula 1 and 2 (both championship and non-championship), Formula 3, Formula Libre, Formula Sport, Grand Touring, Touring Cars, midget racing and karts ! In addition he raced for Audi in the 1980 British Touring Car series and in the American endurance series for road cars, in a

Porsche 944 with Innes Ireland in 1985. Since then he has participated in innumerable historic races since the 70s as part of the vintage brigade. Therefore we do not have room here for a definitive list and one should refer to the statistics from 1947 to 1962 in Robert Edwards' book (see bibliography) which Moss himself reckons is the most accurate source. Here can be found the complete list of Stirling Moss' participation in 66 Grands Prix in the World Championship from 1951 to 1961 inclusive, with a list of the major title and wins in other disciplines and formula. ∎

FORMULA 1_THE 66 GRANDS PRIX

1951_

GRAND PRIX	DATE	CIRCUIT	CAR	QUALIFYING	RACE
1. Switzerland	27 May	Berne-Bremgarten	HWM	14th (2'58''4)	8th

1952_

GRAND PRIX	DATE	CIRCUIT	CAR	QUALIFYING	RACE
1. Switzerland	18 May	Berne-Bremgarten	HWM	9th (2'56''4)	Ret.
2. Belgium	22 June	Spa-Francorchamps	ERA	10th (5'08'')	Ret. (engine)
3. Great Britain	19 July	Silverstone	ERA	16th (1'59'')	Ret. (engine)
4. Holland	17 August	Zandvoort	ERA	18th (nc)	not classified
5. Italy	7 September	Monza	Connaught	9th (2'09''8)	not classified

1953_

GRAND PRIX	DATE	CIRCUIT	CAR	QUALIFYING	RACE
1. Holland	7 June	Zandvoort	Connaught	9th (2'00'')	9th
2. ACF	5 July	Reims	Cooper-Alta	13th (2'55''7)	Ret. (clutch)
3. Germany	2 August	Nürburgring	Cooper-Alta	12th (10'48''3)	6th
4. Italy	13 September	Monza	Cooper-Alta	10th (2'06''6)	not classified

1954_

GRAND PRIX	DATE	CIRCUIT	CAR	QUALIFYING	RACE
1. Belgium	20 June	Spa-Francorchamps	Maserati	10th (4'40''8)	3rd
2. Great Britain	17 July	Silverstone	Maserati	4th (1'47'')	Ret. (gearbox)
FRL with Ascari, Behra, Fangio, Gonzalez, Hawthorn, Marimon: **(1'50''0, 154,159 km/h)**					
3. Germany	1st August	Nürburgring	Maserati	3rd (10'00''7)	Ret. (engine)
4. Switzerland	22 August	Berne-Bremgarten	Maserati	3rd (2'41''4)	Ret. (oil pump)
5. Italy	5 September	Monza	Maserati	3rd (1'59''3)	Ret. (pipe)
6. Spain	24 October	Barcelone-Pedralbes	Maserati	6th (2'21''1)	Ret. (oil pump)

Position in World Championship: 12th / 4 points.   1 fastest race lap.
Average points per race for year: 0.66.

1955_

GRAND PRIX	DATE	CIRCUIT	CAR	QUALIFYING	RACE
1. Argentina	16 January	Buenos Aires	Mercedes	8th (1'44''6)	4th*
2. Monaco	22 May	Monaco	Mercedes	3rd (1'41''2)	10th
3. Belgium	5 June	Spa-Francorchamps	Mercedes	3rd (4'19''2)	2nd
4. Holland	19 June	Zandvoort	Mercedes	2nd (1'40''4)	2nd
5. Great Britain	16 July	Aintree	Mercedes	**Pole (2'00''4)**	**1st** **FRL (2'00''4)**
6. Italy	11 September	Monza	Mercedes	2nd (2'46''8)	Ret. (engine) **FRL (2'46''9)**

(*) Argentina: 1st having taken over the Herrmann and Kling car

Position in World Championship: 2nd / 23 points.   1 pole position, 1 win, 2 fastest race laps.
Average points per race for year: 3.83.

1956_

GRAND PRIX	DATE	CIRCUIT	CAR	QUALIFYING	RACE
1. Argentina	22 January	Buenos Aires	Maserati	7th (1'45''9)	Ret. (engine)
2. Monaco	13 May	Monaco	Maserati	2nd (1'44''6)	**1st**
3. Belgium	3 June	Spa-Francorchamps	Maserati	2nd (4'14''7)	3rd*
4. ACF	1st July	Reims	Maserati	8th (2'29''9)	5th**
5. Great Britain	14 July	Silverstone	Maserati	**Pole (1'41'')**	Ret. (gearbox) **FRL (1'43''2)**
6. Germany	5 August	Nürburgring	Maserati	4th (10'03''4)	2nd
7. Italy	2 September	Monza	Maserati	6th (2'45''9)	**1st** **FRL (2'45''55)**

(*) Belgium: 3rd having taken over Perdisa's car;
(**) ACF: 5th having taken over Perdisa's car.

Position in World Championship: 2nd / 27 points.
Average points per race for year: 3.85. 1 pole position,
2 wins, 2 fastest race laps.

1957_

GRAND PRIX	DATE	CIRCUIT	CAR	QUALIFYING	RACE
1. Argentina	13 January	Buenos Aires	Maserati	**Pole (1'42''6)**	8th **FRL (1'44''7)**
2. Monaco	19 May	Monaco	Vanwall	3rd (1'43''6)	Ret. (accident)
3. Great Britain	20 July	Aintree	Vanwall	**Pole (2'00''4)**	**1st*** **FRL (1'59''2)**
4. Germany	4 August	Nürburgring	Vanwall	7th (9'41''2)	5th
5. Pescara	18 August	Pescara	Vanwall	2nd (9'54''7)	**1st** **FRL (9'44''6)**
6. Italy	8 September	Monza	Vanwall	2nd (1'42''7)	**1st**

(*) Great Britain: 1st having taken over Brooks' car.

Position in World Championship: 2nd / 25 points.
2 pole positions, 3 wins, 3 fastest race laps.
Average points per race for year: 4.16

1958_

GRAND PRIX	DATE	CIRCUIT	CAR	QUALIFYING	RACE
1. Argentina	19 January	Buenos Aires	Cooper-Climax	7th (1'44'')	**1st**
2. Monaco	18 May	Monaco	Vanwall	8th (1'42''3)	Ret. (engine)
3. Holland	26 May	Zandvoort	Vanwall	2nd (1'38'')	**1st** FRL (1'37''6)
4. Belgium	15 June	Spa-Francorchamps	Vanwall	3rd (3'57''6)	Ret. (engine)
5. ACF	6 July	Reims	Vanwall	6th (2'23''7)	2nd
6. Great Britain	19 July	Silverstone	Vanwall	**Pole (1'39''4)**	Ret. (engine)
7. Germany	3 August	Nürburgring	Vanwall	3rd (9'19''1)	Ret. (engine) FRL (9'09''2)
8. Portugal	24 August	Oporto	Vanwall	**Pole (2'34''2)**	**1st**
9. Italy	7 September	Monza	Vanwall	**Pole (1'40''5)**	Ret. (gearbox)
10. Morocco	19 October	Casablanca	Vanwall	2nd (2'23''2)	**1st** FRL (2'22''5)

Position in World Championship: 2nd / 41 points.
3 pole positions, 4 wins, 3 fastest race laps.
Average points per race for year: 4.1.

1959_

GRAND PRIX	DATE	CIRCUIT	CAR	QUALIFYING	RACE
1. Monaco	10 May	Monaco	Cooper-Climax	**Pole (1'39''6)**	Ret. (gearbox)
2. Holland	31 May	Zandvoort	Cooper-Climax	3rd (1'36''2)	Ret. (gearbox) FRL (1'36''6)
3. ACF	5 July	Reims	BRM	4th (2'19''9)	Ret. (accident) FRL (2'22''8)
4. Great Britain	18 July	Aintree	BRM	7th (1'59''6)	2nd FRL (1'57'')
5. Germany	2 August	Avus	Cooper-Climax	2nd (2'06''8)	Ret. (gearbox)
6. Portugal	23 August	Monsanto	Cooper-Climax	**Pole (2'02''89)**	**1st** FRL (2'05''7)
7. Italy	13 September	Monza	Cooper-Climax	**Pole (1'39''7)**	**1st**
8. United States	12 December	Sebring	Cooper-Climax	**Pole (3'00''0)**	Ret. (gearbox)

Position in World Championship: 3rd / 25,5 points.
4 pole positions, 2 wins, 4 fastest race laps.
Average points per race for year: 3.18.

1960_

GRAND PRIX	DATE	CIRCUIT	CAR	QUALIFYING	RACE
1. Argentina	7 February	Buenos Aires	Cooper-Climax	**Pole (1'36''9)**	3rd* FRL (1'38''9)
2. Monaco	29 May	Monaco	Lotus-Climax	**Pole (1'36''3)**	**1st**
3. Holland	6 June	Zandvoort	Lotus-Climax	**Pole (1'33''2)**	4th FRL (1'33''8)
4. Portugal	14 August	Oporto	Lotus-Climax	4th (2'26''19)	Disqualified
5. United States	20 November	Riverside	Lotus-Climax	**Pole (1'54''4)**	**1st**

Position in World Championship: 3rd / 19 points.
Average points per race for year: 3.8.

4 pole positions, 2 wins, 2 fastest race laps.

1961_

GRAND PRIX	DATE	CIRCUIT	CAR	QUALIFYING	RACE
1. Monaco	14 May	Monaco	Lotus-Climax	**Pole (1'39''1)**	**1st** FRL (with Ginther) (1'36''3)
2. Holland	22 May	Zandvoort	Lotus-Climax	4th (1'36''2)	4th
3. Belgium	18 June	Spa-Francorchamps	Lotus-Climax	8th (4'08''2)	8th
4. ACF	2 July	Reims	Lotus-Climax	4th (2'27''6)	Ret. (brakes)
5. Great Britain	15 July	Aintree	Lotus-Climax	5th (1'59'')	Ret. (brakes)
6. Germany	6 August	Nürburgring	Lotus-Climax	3rd (9'01''4)	**1st**
7. Italy	10 September	Monza	Lotus-Climax	11th (2'51''8)	Ret. (bearing)
8. United States	8 October	Watkins Glen	Lotus-Climax	3rd (1'18''2)	Ret. (bearing) FRL (1'18''2)

Position in World Championship: 3rd / 21 points.
1 pole position, 2 wins, 2 fastest race laps.
Average points per race for year: 2.625.

MAJOR WINS IN NON-CHAMPIONSHIP FORMULA 1 RACES

1954

COUNTRY	DATE	RACE	CIRCUIT	CAR	
G.-B.	29 May	200 Miles	Aintree	Maserati 250 F	
G.-B.	7 August	Gold Cup	Oulton Park	Maserati 250 F	FRL
G.-B.	25 September	Goodwood Trophy	Goodwood	Maserati 250 F	FRL
G.-B.	2nd October	Daily Telegraph Trophy	Aintree	Maserati 250 F	FRL

1955

COUNTRY	DATE	RACE	CIRCUIT	CAR	
G.-B.	24 September	Gold Cup	Oulton Park	Maserati 250 F	FRL

1956

COUNTRY	DATE	RACE	CIRCUIT	CAR	
NZ	7 January	New Zealand GP	Ardmore	Maserati 250 F	FRL
G.-B.	2nd April	Glover Trophy	Goodwood	Maserati 250 F	FRL
G.-B.	23 April	200 Miles	Aintree	Maserati 250 F	
G.-B.	5 May	International Trophy	Silverstone	Vanwall	FRL
G.B.	21 May	London Trophy	Crystal Palace	Maserati 250 F	FRL
AUS	2nd December	Australian GP	Melbourne	Maserati 250 F	FRL

1958

COUNTRY	DATE	RACE	CIRCUIT	CAR	
G.-B.	19 April	200Miles	Aintree	Cooper-Climax 1,9 l.	
F	20 July	Caen GP	Caen	Cooper-Climax 2,2 l.	
DK	15 August	Copenhagen GP	Roskilde	JBW-Maserati	
AUS	29 November	Melbourne GP	Albert Park	Cooper-Climax 2 l.	FRL

1959

COUNTRY	DATE	RACE	CIRCUIT	CAR	
G.-B.	26 September	Gold Cup	Oulton Park	Cooper-Climax 2,5 l.	FRL
USA	18 October	GP Formule Libre	Watkins Glen	Cooper-Climax 2,5 l.	FRL

1960

COUNTRY	DATE	RACE	CIRCUIT	CAR	
G.-B.	24 September	Gold Cup	Oulton Park	Lotus-Climax 18	FRL
USA	9 October	GP Formule Libre	Watkins Glen	Lotus-Climax 18	FRL

1961

COUNTRY	DATE	RACE	CIRCUIT	CAR	
AUS	29 January	Australian GP	Warwick Farm (Sydney)	Lotus-Climax 18	FRL
A	16 April	Vienna GP	Aspern	Lotus-Climax 18	FRL
S	20 August	Kannonlopet	Karlskoga	Lotus-Climax 18/21	FRL
DK	27 August	Danish GP	Roskildering	Lotus-Climax 18/21	FRL
I	3rd September	Modena GP	Modène	Lotus-Climax 18/21	FRL
G.-B.	23 September	Gold Cup	Oulton Park	Ferguson-Climax P 99	(only race win for a 4 wheel drive Formula 1 car)

1962

COUNTRY	DATE	RACE	CIRCUIT	CAR	
NZ	6 January	New Zealand GP	Ardmore	Lotus-Climax 212,5 l.	MTC
NZ	20 January	Lady Wigram Trophy	Christchurch	Lotus-Climax 212,5 l.	MTC

MAJOR WINS IN FORMULA 2

1951

COUNTRY	DATE	RACE	CIRCUIT	CAR	
G.-B.	29 September	Madgwick Cup	Goodwood	HWM	FRL
G.-B.	13 October	Winfield Races	Ecosse	HWM	FRL

1953

COUNTRY	DATE	RACE	CIRCUIT	CAR	
G.-B.	19 September	London Trophy	Crystal Palace	Cooper-Alta	FRL

1958

COUNTRY	DATE	RACE	CIRCUIT	CAR	
G.-B.	30 August	Kentish 100	Brands Hatch	Cooper-Climax F2	FRL

1959

COUNTRY	DATE	RACE	CIRCUIT	CAR	
I	25 April	Syracuse GP	Sicily	Cooper-Borgward F2	
F	5 July	Coupe de Vitesse	Reims-Gueux	Cooper-Borgward F2	FRL
F	12 July	GP de Rouen	Rouen-les-Essarts	Cooper-Borgward F2	FRL
F	26 July	Circuit d'Auvergne	Charade	Cooper-Borgward F2	FRL

1960

COUNTRY	DATE	RACE	CIRCUIT	CAR	
B	10 April	200 Miles	Aintree	Porsche F2	
A	18 September	Austrian GP	Zeltweg	Porsche F2	FRL
AF	17 December	Cape GP	Killarney	Porsche F2	
AF	27 December	South African	East London	Porsche F2	

MAJOR WINS IN FORMULA 3

1948_

COUNTRY	DATE	RACE	CIRCUIT	CAR		
G.-B.	18 September	(inauguration of circuit)	Goodwood	Cooper-Jap 500 Mk II		

1949_

G.-B.	14 May	(GP curtain raiser)	Silverstone	Cooper-Jap 500 Mk III	FRL	

1950_

MC	20 May	(Monaco GP curtain raiser)		Cooper-JAP 500 Mk IV	FRL	

1951_

G.-B.	14 July	Race 500*	Silverstone	Kieft-Norton	FRL	
NL	22 July	Race 500*	Zandvoort	Kieft-Norton	FRL	

1952_

G.-B.	19 July	Race 500*	Silverstone	Kieft-Norton	FRL	

1953_

D	31 May	Eifelrennen 500	Nürburgring	Cooper-Norton 500 Mk VII		*(GP curtain raiser)

MAJOR WINS IN SPORTS CARS AND GT

1950_

COUNTRY	DATE	RACE	CIRCUIT	CAR		
EIR	16 September	RAC Tourist Trophy	Dundrod	Jaguar XK 120		

1951_

G.-B.	14 June	British Empire Trophy	Douglas (Isle of Man)	Frazer-Nash	FRL	
EIR	15 September	RAC Tourist Trophy	Dundrod	Jaguar XK 120 C		

1952_

G.-B.	10 May	Race of Champions	Silverstone	Jaguar XK 120		
F	29 June	GP de la Marne	Reims-Gueux	Jaguar XK 120 C		

1953_

F	5 July	12 Heures de Reims	Reims-Gueux	Jaguar XK 120 C		(codriver: Peter Whitehead)

1954_

USA	7 March	Sebring 12 Hours	Sebring (Florida)	Osca 1500		(codriver: Bill Lloyd)

1955_

I	1st May	Mille Miglia		Mercedes 300 SLR		(navigator: Denis Jenkinson) OUTRIGHT RECORD FOR EVENT
PG	24 July	Governor's Trophy	Lisbon	Porsche 550	FRL	
EIR	19 September	RAC Tourist Trophy	Dundrod	Mercedes 300 SLR	FRL	(codriver: John Fitch)
I	16 October	Targa Florio	Sicily	Mercedes 300 SLR	FRL	(codriver: Peter Collins)

1956_

D	27 May	1000 Km of the Nürburgring		Maserati 300 S		(codriver: Jean Behral)
G.-B.	14 July	(GP curtain raiser)	Silverstone	Maserati 300 S	FRL	
V	4 November	Venezuela Sport GP	Caracas	Maserati 300 S		
AUS	25 November	Australian Tourist Trophy	Albert Park (Melbourne)	Maserati 300 S	FRL	

1957_

S	11 August	Swedish Sport Grand Prix	Rabelov	Maserati 450 S		(codrivers: Jean Behra, Harry Schell)

1958_

C	23 February	Cugan Sport GP	La Havane (circuit El Malecon)	Ferrari 335 S		
D	1st June	1000 Km of the Nürburgring		Aston Martin DBR 1	FRL	(codriver: Jack Brabham)
PG	13 July	GP Sport de Vila Real		Maserati 300 S	FRL	
G.-B.	19 July	(GP curtain raiser)	Silverstone	Lister-Jaguar	FRL	
G.-B.	13 September	RAC Tourist Trophy	Goodwood	Aston Martin DBR 1	FRL	(codriver: Tony Brooks)

1959_

COUNTRY	DATE	RACE	CIRCUIT	CAR	
G.-B.	2nd May	RACE GT	Silverstone	Aston Martin DB 4 GT	FRL
D	7 June	1000 Km of the Nürburgring		Aston Martin DBR 1	FRL *(codriver: Jack Fairman)*
F	12 July	Coupe Delamarre-Deboutteville		Maserati Tipo 60 "Birdcage"	FRL
PG	23 August	Portuguese Sport GP		Cooper-Monaco	FRL
G.-B.	5 September	RAC Tourist Trophy	Goodwood		*(codriver: Tony Brooks ; taking over the sister car of Shelby-Fairman after a fire)*
USA	27 Nov./4 Dec.	Governor's Trophy		Aston Martin DB 4 GT	FRL
				Aston Martin DBR 2	FRL

1960_

COUNTRY	DATE	RACE	CIRCUIT	CAR	
C	28 February	GP Sport de Cuba	La Havane (circuit El Malecon)	Maserati Tipo 61	FRL
D	22 May	1000 Km du Nürburgring	Nürburgring	Maserati Tipo 61 "Birdcage"	FRL *(codriver: Dan Gurney)*
S	7 August	Kannonlopet	Karskoga	Lotus-Climax 19 "Monte Carlo"	FRL
G.-B.	20 August	RAC Tourist Trophy	Goodwood	Ferrari 250 GT	FRL

1961_

COUNTRY	DATE	RACE	CIRCUIT	CAR
G.-B.	19 August	RAC Tourist Trophy	Goodwood	Ferrari 250 GT

TOURING CARS AND RALLIES

1952, 1953 and 1954_

COUNTRY	DATE	RACE	CIRCUIT	CAR	
G.-B.	May races	"Production"	Silverstone	Jaguar Mk VII	FRL
DIV	July	Coupe des Alpes		Sunbeam-Talbot	
		Coupe d'or des Alpes		*(codriver: John Cutts)*	

RECORDS

1950_

COUNTRY	DATE	CIRCUIT	CAR		
F	21 November	Anneau de Montlhéry	Kieft-Norton 350 cc	6 records Class J	
F	23 November	Anneau de Montlhéry	Kieft-Norton 500 cc	7 records Class I	*(codrivers: Ken Gregory and Jack Neill)*

1952_

F	5-12 August	Anneau de Montlhéry	Jaguar XK 120 coupé	5 distance records	*(codrivers: Leslie Johnson, Jack Fairman, Bert Hadley)*

1956_

I	3 September	Anneau de Monza	Lotus-Climax 11	2 records (50 km ; 50 miles)

1957_

USA	23 August	Salt Lake, Bonneville, Utah	MG EX 181	5 international records

ABBREVIATIONS_

A:	Austria	DIV	Diverse	I:	Italy	S:	Sweden
AF:	Africa	DK:	Denmark	MC:	Monaco	USA:	United States of America
AUS:	Australia	EIR:	Northern Ireland	NL:	Netherland	V:	Venezuela
B:	Belgium	F:	France	NZ:	New Zealand		
C:	Cuba	FRL:	Fastest Race Lap	PG:	Portugal		
D:	Germany	G.-B.:	Great Britain	Ret.:	Retirement		

INDEX

159

_WITH THANKS TO

Christian Bedeï, Tony Brooks, Bernard Cahier, Cyril Davillerd, Luc Domenjoz, Sébastien Dulac, Robert Edwards, Ken Gregory, Robert Manzon, Christian Moity, Stirling and Susie Moss, Pat Moss-Carlsson, Johnny Rives, Vincent Souchaud, John Surtees, Rob Walker
With special thanks to Sylvie (JV)

_BIBLIOGRAPHY

BOOKS ABOUT STIRLING MOSS
"All but my life", by Stirling Moss and Ken W. Purdy, William Kimber, 1963
"My cars, my career ", by Stirling Moss and Doug Nye, Haynes Publishing, 1987, revised. 1999
"Stirling Moss – Racing with the maestro", by Karl Ludwigsen, Patrick Stephens Ltd., 1997
"Stirling Moss – The authorized biography", by Robert Edwards, Cassell & Co, 2000

OTHER TITLES
"Challenge me the race", by Mike Hawthorn, Aston Publications, London 1958
"Historique de la course automobile – 1894-1978", by Edmond Cohin, Editions Larivière, coll. Le Fanauto, Paris 1978
"World Champion", by John Surtees, Hazlandon Publishing, London 1991
"The Great Encyclopedia of Formula one", 1950-2000", by Pierre Ménard, Editions Chronosports, Lausanne 2000
"Time and two seats – Five decades of long-distance racing", by Janos L. Wimpffen, Motorsport Research Group, Redmond (WA-USA) 1999.